Unleashing the Pro in PROject Management: The Ambitious Project Manager's Guide to Personal and Professional Mastery

ISBN: 978-0-6457998-1-1

Disclaimer

The material in this publication is of the nature of general comment only, and does not represent professional advice. It is not intended to provide specific guidance for particular circumstances and it should not be relied on as the basis for any decision to take action or not take action on any matter which it covers.

Readers should obtain professional advice where appropriate, before making any such decision.

To the maximum extent permitted by law, the author and publisher disclaim all responsibility and liability to any person, arising directly or indirectly from any person taking or not taking action based on the information in this publication.

Dedication

I dedicate this book to the people in my life who have not only been influential in bringing my purpose to life but, more importantly, have always supported and encouraged me to follow my dreams.

To Mamma (Teresa) and Pappa (Frank) Coco

- without you both, I would never have existed. I thank you for making the decision to migrate to Australia to pursue your own dream for a better life. The way you have loved, cared for, and nurtured me as your son has become part of who I am as an individual. And your values, integrity, and commitment to being hardworking and honest parents have set the foundations for how I live my life. I am the product of the love you had for each other, and I thank you for your unconditional love and support as you watched me grow into a man on a mission to live his own dreams. All my love to you both forever!

To Phuong Phan, the founder of the School of Purpose

- from the moment we met, you have always been there for me as a friend, soul-sister, and coach. You have helped me not only grow as a person but also grow professionally—to come out of my shell and believe in my purpose. You have taught me the importance of dedication and perseverance in my pursuit of making a difference in this world.

This book is a by-product of your support as a "midwife" responsible for helping me birth my vision of a community that has come into this world called the "Project Managers Movement". You have been a big supporter and one of my most trusted advisors. And you have always believed in me, even when I did not believe in myself. I am a better person overall because of you. Thank you for everything.

To Sam Cawthorn, the CEO of Speakers Institute

- since I met you, I knew you would become a significant influence in my life. And more importantly, you would inspire me with your own story and way of being, allowing me to believe that my own dreams were possible, too. You have helped me become a more confident, passionate, and professional speaker. And you have taught me how to connect with my audience, deliver my message with clarity and passion, and leverage my vision. This has inspired me to continue to deliver my own legacy to the world.

You have been my mentor, my coach, my guide, my friend, and one of my biggest supporters. You have always believed in me, which has provided me the motivation to keep going in my pursuit of my own dreams. I am a better speaker and a better person because of you. Thank you.

To my gorgeous wife, Tiffany

- You are the most beautiful part of my world. The woman who provides me not only with tough love when I need it but also strategic pieces of advice when I am out on my entrepreneurial adventures. And I definitely need your gentle reminders to take care of myself while I am on my mission to help others.

You are kind, compassionate, intelligent, creative, and funny. You are my best friend, my lover, and my soulmate. I could not have made it this far without you, and the decision to finally write this book was something you have always encouraged me to do. You have been my outright biggest supporter and my most trusted advisor. You have always believed in me, even when I haven't always believed in myself. You have always encouraged me to follow my dreams. And you have always been there to pick me up when I have fallen, which has been the case many times over.

I am so grateful to have you in my life. You make me a better man. You inspire me to be the best version of myself. I love you more than words could ever express. Always and forever.

Last but not least, this book is especially dedicated to... YOU!

The project managers (aspiring & seasoned) and ALL other supporting project management roles, the corporate leaders and employees who are dedicated and committed to what they do professionally, sometimes to the detriment of your own health and well-being. I want you to find inspiration and motivation in this book to not only excel and enjoy your role in project management, but also to understand that if we ALL come together, share our experiences, and acknowledge that project management is a TEAM sport, we can refine our craft and reap the rewards so we can live a fulfilling life as we work in this wonderful profession.

I find it wonderful to know that my own "pain and suffering" was not wasted in sharing my experiences and learnings in my own journey in this book. Hopefully, it will help hundreds and thousands of people—including YOU—to NOT make the same mistakes that I did, allowing you to progress and flourish in your own journey towards self-mastery!

Thank you for making the decision to read my book.

Sincerely,

Leo Coco

Get Goosebumps when I think back on the session

I know the line is cliche but honestly can't describe in words how thrilled I was to receive such an amazing coaching session on the 30th morning. Every single moment of that session was a thrilling experience. Looking forward for more such sessions - **Nadene**

—

Group Coaching Session - What an Experience of a Lifetime!

I have been part of the PPM community for almost 2 years and six months as a coaching student of Leo. Every meet up and session with Leo is incredible, he is such a friendly and caring person that you won't forget and you would always look forward to experiencing again. - **Hiren Parmar**

—

My experience with Project Managers Movement

I went along to a Project Manager Movement meeting, as a networking opportunity. What I found was a group of engaging individuals that were willing to include and embrace new members. This culture is testament to Leo's style of organising and commitment to developing a true movement in his industry, where he knows first hand about the emotional and stress levels of project managers. - **Paul Brooke**

—

Superb Leo

Leo is the awesome man behind the PMM community which helps numerous project management professionals as well as project management students to learn about new trends in the field. Also it is a very good community for like minded people where we share and learn and build a network. Best of luck Leo for this great initiative. - **Kush Jindal**

—

Positive and Beautiful community

Having spent time with this beautifully diverse group, I really felt the openness and sincerity of the people in the community. Kudos to our leader and organizer Leo Coco whose heart to help and develop people has made the Project Management Movement a place where you can build meaningful relationships, both in the personal and professional level. Hope to see you there one day. - **Chris Calixto**

—

Unleashing the Pro in PROject Management

The Ambitious Project Manager's Guide to Personal and Professional Mastery

Leo Coco

Table of Contents

Foreword

Leo is one of the most charismatic people I've ever met and he's one of the most courageous. The uniqueness of his life, lifestyle, family dynamics, startup challenges and professional success is a reflection of the conscious choices he's made to do things differently.

It is my pleasure to introduce this work to readers and to offer a few thoughts on what they can expect to find within its pages. Whether you are an avid reader seeking a new adventure, a scholar in search of new insights in the field of corporate management and entrepreneurship, or simply curious about the world around you, this book promises to deliver an engaging and informative experience.

The topics covered in this work will help you venture into the world of project management.

Each chapter offers a unique perspective and a fresh set of ideas, all presented in a clear and accessible style that invites readers to explore and reflect on their own situation, whether it be personal or professional. Leo is a world-class operator, not merely an armchair philosopher.

Please take action and be cautious of the wind. The ideas shared in this book may be simple, but the application of the core principles can be potent.

As a Spiritual and Business Coach and advisor for over twenty years and founder of the School of Purpose, I am delighted to have played a role in Leo's fascinating and successful journey.

With the turn of EVERY page of this book, I found myself reflecting and checking if I have taken his techniques on board. Leo's challenges that he shares from his life, are the key secret to succeeding when the universe throws the big obstacles at you. My hope is this book will inspire and inform readers, and that it will serve as a catalyst for further exploration and discovery.

So without further ado, I invite you to turn the page and embark on this journey of discovery with an open mind and a sense of curiosity. May this book enrich your understanding of the world and ignite your passion for learning.

Phuong B. T. Phan

CHAPTER 1

Shaping One's Beliefs

If there's one thing Frank knew best, it was how to be a hard worker.

He'd work full shifts 7 days a week for a carpet manufacturer. At home, he worked equally hard to provide his family with whatever they needed.

He'd bring home every last penny he made to his family. He'd sit at the dinner table, telling stories and jokes packed with life lessons. He even grew fruit and vegetables in the backyard for the family to enjoy!

Perhaps, that last one was also his way of staying connected to his roots. See, before moving to Australia and becoming Frank, the labourer, he was known as Francesco, the young farm boy in Sicily. He couldn't finish school back in his motherland, but he brought with him clear beliefs about working hard... avoiding risks... saving money... and conforming to "acceptable" behaviour so as not to draw much attention.

Teresa, Frank's wife, is his perfect match. A hard worker herself, she worked in the "Rag Trade" as an incredible dressmaker. She worked from home in a downstairs office, making sample dresses for various designers. She'd be up before the sun rose, and would work long after it had gone down. On top of that, she cooked, cleaned, and took care of the cat with hardly any complaints. She'd been at it since she and Frank immigrated to Australia in the late 1950s.

One Wednesday morning, Frank and Teresa were at the Balmain Hospital in New South Wales, having the time of their lives—for the second time around. They gave birth to a boy—the last addition to their small family of four.

That boy was me.

I was brought home shortly after, and just like that—I was part of a household with my parents and sister, Rose, who was six years old at the time.

I have fond memories of my childhood.

I remember watching my dad tend to the garden as I listened to stories from when he was young.

Day after day, I'd wake up at the crack of dawn, thinking I had finally "beaten" my mum by getting out of bed before she did... but every day without fail, I'd go downstairs and see she's already hard at work making dresses.

We'd send my sister to school, and I distinctly remember the excitement of going to school and being able to learn from these wise, old people I knew as "teachers."

Little did I know that I was subconsciously building my way of thinking and my whole sense of self around all these "big" people around me. Little did I know back then that I would slowly inherit their beliefs, cultures, and ways of living. And little did I know that even my eyes digested and consumed the world around me, without my even meaning to!

See, people often get surprised that I was very hardworking and domesticated. I never used to help mum cook or clean, and I left Dad to do his gardening, but when I left home I was just able to do all of it. Just watching that stuff happen every day at home meant that it was ingrained in me. In fact, I attribute most of my personality to my mum, whose energetic, and go-getter personality just rubbed off on me growing up!

But aside from what I subconsciously inherited from the adults who helped raise me... I also remember that I was explicitly taught some behaviours which I still consciously enact to this day.

See, whether I was heading to school or visiting a relative's house with my parents and sister... I would always be briefed in advance on how I should act.

Stay seated unless you're told otherwise.

Do not take any food or treats if offered, unless I give you permission.

Raise your hand if you want to say something, and don't speak until you're asked to.

All these rules were quite confusing for a young kid who wants to interact and discover, but nonetheless, I complied. There was always a sense of having to abide by the rules… whether they were created by my parents or my teachers at school.

And because of those simple directives which I thought nothing of at the time… I grew up to be the kind of guy who stands back and is always the last person to get up to get food at a buffet.

My wife, Tiffany, is the exact opposite. She'd drag me to the front of the buffet line and lecture me about how we needed to get food first. She'd even finish her serving before the last of the guests got theirs!

Of course, just like mine, Tiffany's behaviour was shaped by rules—both formal and unwritten—that she was taught as a young girl.

See, she was brought up in an environment where she had to fend for herself. When a big dish of food would get put in the middle of their dinner table, if you weren't fast, you ate last. That's why she thought it was absurd that I'd stand back and be the last one to get up for food. And I bet if you asked Tiffany's parents and siblings, they'd think the same.

All these experiences made me realise that we all live by different rules, depending on the things we were exposed to and were taught growing up.

Rules, Rules, and More Rules

It was fair to say that as I was growing up, it felt like life was made up of many rules for many different situations.

And I know it's not just me.

From the moment we are born, all of us are subjected to various forms of conditioning from our parents, school, and the media.

Just think of how almost everyone seems to have a similar idea of what success looks like. It's becoming a top-level executive at a firm... and having a big house that you share with your spouse, two children, and a golden retriever or two.

How did we all come up with this idea?

Well, you'd observe that every major private school teaches its students... that intelligence is one of the most important things and one of the measures of future success. So, what the school does is it trains you how to think logically and analytically to solve problems. It doesn't train you to be entirely creative in your thinking, nor does it encourage you to take risks or even consider the world of business and entrepreneurship. We are instead groomed for conservative, safe, white collar jobs that can help us *feel* prestigious or important.

And since we're put under pressure to pick the career or job we'd be doing for the rest of our lives at the young age of 18, many of us pretty much get stuck. Ultimately, this conditioning urges us to look for a job, stay the course, and stick to the status quo.

But while I'm a product of so many rules myself, there have always been a lot of questions at the back of my head:

Why are there so many rules to follow in every situation we find ourselves in?

And, more importantly...

Why should all these rules be as simple as the Ten Commandments of Catholicism, which are considered divine law because God himself supposedly revealed them?

Should these be the true guiding principles for my life?

Am I really supposed to subscribe with the other overarching belief instilled in Catholics about these commandments?

"Obey them and eternal happiness is yours. Disobey them and suffer the consequences."

I guess it's pretty clear that as we progress through adulthood, the carefree spirit and playful nature of childhood are left behind. As I've said earlier, all I wanted as a child was to interact and discover, but instead, I was told to keep quiet and hold back.

Imagine all the times you had a million questions running through your mind but were trained to sit in silence instead. I've been there. And that's how many of us shift from being talkative, inquisitive kids… to adults who have a hard time participating in discussions unless directly called to speak.

Now, wouldn't you agree that since there were so many rules for us to abide by… it felt like we were forced to go through this thing called LIFE with so much thinking and complexity… when we should just be living it?

The Power of the Mind

Everything that has happened to us up to this point really has an impact on how we think, which turns into our beliefs.

You'd notice so many people in your life trying to give advice based on their personal experiences in chasing happiness. It then becomes obvious that people's stories reflect how they behave through life, which is normally based on what they believed. See, the stories we tell ourselves to be true and the things we believe to be true about the world around us… will deeply influence how we live.

And if you're not careful, you might end up picking up mindsets and behaviours that do not serve the kind of life you want to live.

That's because the mind is a powerful thing. It will digest everything it is fed… and it cannot, by itself, distinguish between the good and bad information. It will simply take in everything you expose it to. And these beliefs can either prevent you from having a fulfilling life or allow your world to blossom.

For instance... if you spend most of your time with a pessimist who's always talking about how the world is soon going to end... you might lose your drive to make monumental changes in your life.

Why bother, you might ask, *when we're all just going to die soon?*

But if you switch things up and surround yourself with people who are always talking about the beauty of the mundane... you'll eventually have this belief that every moment of life is meant to be savoured and lived fully. And that might influence you to create meaningful changes in your life.

I've personally discovered a strong link between my beliefs and my behaviours. Even as a young adult, I was starting to feel like I had been programmed to live life a certain way. And that's by using the beliefs and values which I had formed through my cultural background, community, local laws, and societal rulings... along with the things I had previously learned from my parents and teachers. All the things I was taught became apparent in my behaviour and even in the way I communicated with people.

Overall, I've formed habits based on deeply-held beliefs. Some of these habits serve me in a positive way and propel me forward. Unfortunately, some also kept me stuck where I am for a long time, holding me back from living life the way I would have wanted to.

Fortunately, and although it's a little late... I learned how to unlearn some of those bad habits that were formed from rules and beliefs I never should have subscribed to. And I'd be the first to tell you that some habits are really hard to break. It would have been easier if I had questioned those rules and beliefs in the first place... so that I never formed habits around them at all.

After all, some of the rules I grew up abiding by are what Vishen Lakhiani would refer to as "bullshit rules."

Exercise 1: BRULES

Vishen Lakhiani, the CEO of Mindvalley and the author of *The Code of the Extraordinary Mind,* coined a term for limiting rules:

He called them "BRULES," short for "bullshit rules."

Lakhiani understood very well that as people, we all absorb the cultural norms and rules of society. So much so, that we often forget to question whether these "brules" are serving us... or limiting us in life.

That's why we need to train our minds to be aware of our beliefs, especially since there are a lot of things we don't even *know* we believe in.

So now, let's take a page out of Lakhiani's book and do an exercise that will help you become more aware of some "brules" you may be living by.

Take the time to stop for a moment and write down on a piece of paper all the "bullshit rules" you're subscribed to, which may or may not be serving you.

This might include rules that others have placed on you... like the type of job you should have. Or the amount of risk you should take in life. Or even the number of "investment properties" you're supposed to have at this point in your life.

Then, think long and hard about what habits you may have formed due to your previous acceptance of these "rules."

Here's a hypothetical example:

Well-meaning parents pass down to their children the idea that if you want to be successful, you will have to do some hard work. But that doesn't mean you should spend 60-80 hours each week doing work you don't care about. And it doesn't mean you have to sacrifice other aspects of your life to get ahead in your career. Working smart is often more important than working hard.

Take 5 minutes to brainstorm and write down as many "brules" and habits that you can think of which could be limiting you from achieving what you want in life.

After that, come back and think about how you could change those beliefs or upgrade (see: quit) those habits... in a way that serves you and allows you to grow.

Take Control of Your Life

It is worth repeating that the mind is a powerful thing.

It has the capability to absorb everything you observe in the real world around you.

But that doesn't mean you're completely vulnerable to the people and rule-making institutions you're exposed to.

Always remember that the mind has a filter—and that's your consciousness. What you consciously decide to believe in and what you consciously decide to do... will always be ingrained in your life deeper than what you subconsciously consume.

So, while you may not be able to stop your mind from absorbing everything it's fed, ultimately, YOU can decide what beliefs and rules you live your life by.

You could even surround yourself with more people whose habits you want to have in your life. After all, you already know that it is our beliefs that influence our behaviour and the way we live. Hence, you can take control of your life by exposing yourself to environments that allow you to create new beliefs that can help you grow and move forward.

At the same time, you can keep on doing Lakhiani's exercise above to help purge your life of "brules" that are not serving you and the purpose you've set for yourself in life.

That's how you can make sure that all these "rules" you're supposed to follow are not actually holding you back from living life the way you want.

What I Learned From Running an IT Consulting Business: RESPONSIBILITY

I've always had a passion for business, borne out of a drive of doing things for myself. The idea of creating and being in control of my own destiny was exciting for me. I am deeply in tune with my entrepreneurial spirit, which allows me to be creative, experimental, and take risks.

So in 1997, I registered my first business name as a sole trader and embarked on a journey which I was yet to understand at the time. That became the most significant platform for my learning in IT & Project Management, but it also provided me with a profound insight to self-discovery through delivering IT consulting, support services, and project management to the marketplace.

Working hard came naturally to me with the upbringing that I had, having worked from the age of 11 doing newspaper runs... if you're old enough to remember those days. I then progressed to working at the Golden Arches (McDonalds) and quickly moved up to a team leadership role.

Driven by my desire, excitement, and the unknown of doing something different, I broke the mould of the usual 9 to 5 grind we were all conditioned to do.

As I started this business from humble beginnings of just building desktop computers for customers, my first lesson was just around the corner from me: RESPONSIBILITY.

As is the case in the corporate world, the most prominent reason used for failure, especially when delivering projects... is blaming someone or something else to make us feel better about ourselves or the situation.

But as it was my own business, I suddenly had nowhere to hide. When one of my custom PC builds failed, it was difficult to make excuses for the failure.

I found myself getting more and more responsible over time, thanks to these experiences of failure. Those situations were and continue to be my greatest learning experiences in life... as they have become an opportunity for growth as an individual.

TIP: Failure is part of learning which I embraced, and I encourage you to do it, too. When you accept this as part of the process of growth, it becomes the most empowering mindset shift you can make in your life. It can support you as you try new things, explore new beliefs, and take on new habits.

CHAPTER 2

Who Am I & Why You Should Listen To Me

In my 20+ years in Project and Program Management, I have seen and learned so much.

I have been given both misguided information and invaluable knowledge that stretched me to grow beyond what I thought was possible.

But fundamentally, the experiences I've had inspired, taught, and even tried to break me.

This challenged me to continue believing in myself, and encourage my teams to have fun while also delivering major technology transformations to my customers.

I have completed a multitude of professional development certifications for Project Management. These have shown their value over the years being used in both solo and hybrid modes:

- ITIL Foundations
- Prince2 Certified Practitioner
- Certified Scrum Master
- Lean Six Sigma Yellow Belt
- Agile Project Management Practitioner
- Certified Data Centre Migration Specialist
- Managing Successful Programmes Practitioner

Having had the opportunity to work with some of the biggest multinational organisations and system integrators in Australia, including Coca-Cola, Qantas Airways, Woolworths, Fujitsu, Telstra, Google, and Cisco... one thing was for sure: All the training and certifications I had in various Project Management frameworks and methodologies definitely helped me succeed.

But it also became obvious that there are things left to be learned on the job.

The problem is that when you are under lots of pressure, sometimes it doesn't take much for projects to turn into extremely stressful situations.

This triggers our brain to move from logic to impulse.

That means if our brain detects any type of perceived threat, it can go into the "fight-or-flight" mode BEFORE we've had a chance to consciously review the situation. This then reduces our ability to think clearly, which can result in worse outcomes during a crisis situation.

Ironically, it is when you face these difficult situations that you need your brain to be working at its best... so that you can keep your perspective of what is important.

I definitely will never forget when I was put in a situation with a client that triggered this exact "fight-or-flight" response in me:

I was asked to manage an account for an enterprise customer after the sudden resignation of the account manager. Here, I found myself already challenged running a complex initiative. And now, I was given the added responsibility of being an account manager with just a five minutes' notice. It was an awful feeling. I felt this heat come over my body—it felt like I was going to have a heart attack!

While I did survive the ordeal, the physical and mental impact of that situation was life-changing. It made me realise how people and culture within an organisation play a significant part in the performance of its employees and teams.

But if that's the case, why do we see a lot of leadership teams use dictatorship and intimidation techniques to get projects delivered? How can we go about winning friends and influencing people so that we can deliver our projects? What's the most effective way to deal with conflict so that it does not prevent your project from progressing?

There were many questions but not too many answers at the time. So, we persevered and just got the job done.

Another thing that is blatantly obvious for many people coming into the Project Management industry is this:

Getting that first entry-level role is never easy. Although the marketplace needs great people, it's still difficult to find your first break... unless you get handed a lucky break, or you create your own.

The Project Managers Movement Community

As the Founder of a Professional Community of Project Delivery Professionals, Corporate Leaders and Employees, I created Project Managers Movement (PMM).

This was a dream brought to life through my personal development and the spiritual work I do with Phuong Phan, the founder of the School of Purpose. Within 6 months of working with Phuong, PMM was born. And now, I use this as a platform to inspire, share insights and stories, and also help aspiring project management professionals to get started in the industry.

Project Managers Movement is a safe, non-judgmental community that works with project delivery professionals... corporate leaders... and employees, helping them embrace their uniqueness and focus on self-mastery through personal & professional development.

As I move towards realising my 2030 Vision for Project Managers Movement... I imagine the value that this community continues to bring to its members... through the forming of relationships that feel like family... knowledge sharing and storytelling... being vulnerable, and sharing your failures and fears... while also being connected to industry professionals and a supportive culture like no other.

It's just priceless to have people who will cheer you on as you dare to dream and focus on your own self-mastery.

The Value of Effective Communication

Part of being a project delivery professional involves being able to communicate effectively with your customers, teams, and stakeholders at all levels. The words we speak tell us much about what we are thinking. Thus, our language has a tremendous influence on the results of both our projects and the way that our relationships with our teams and stakeholders develop.

Now, as a Professional & Public Speaker and a Speakers Institute Certified Coach, I look back at the many wonderful things I have learnt and continue to learn from my mentor Sam Cawthorn, the Founder and CEO of Speakers Institute.

Sam has a vision, and an immense presence on and off stage which is infectious and that caught me many years ago. I am now in the proximity of incredible people who are also taking their messages to the world, which will over time see a change in the world for the better.

I use my own learnings in communication and speech, combined with an authorised training curriculum... to teach Project Delivery Professionals the skills needed to master their communication. This allows them to have influence in the workplace... deliver impactful presentations... and master non-verbal communication techniques as part of their professional craft.

In October 2020, I had the privilege of completing the Power Voice Certificate Online Coaching Program with another of my mentors, who is also one of the greatest Motivational Speakers on this planet, Les Brown.

Les shared his insights and learnings. But what I valued the most is his passion for helping people and really making a difference in their lives. He is one of the most powerful and inspiring forces I have in my proximity.

My encounters with so many professional speakers made me realise something:

Ineffective communication contributes to so many issues within projects... and adds a layer of risk when making organisational decisions.

See, when you have the words, and you can tell stories that move someone to feel, you have an opportunity to influence those around you.

And it is known that a significant amount of the time in a project is spent on communication by the project manager. So, we can say that communication is like the project's lifeblood – as everything in a project is ultimately based on how efficiently we communicate with our team, stakeholders, and users.

What I Learned From Running an IT Consulting Business: CONFIDENCE

It was incredible how comfortable I became with having failure as part of running my business.

See, I used to be extremely fearful of delivering those PCs to customers, always anxious about something going wrong.

Now, I have shifted my mindset that if a PC build fails, I just have to accept it as part of the process. Instead of moping around and feeling bad for myself when things went wrong, I simply focused on finding solutions. When I accepted failure as part of the process… it was amazing how confident I became and ultimately also mastered resolving the issues quickly.

Maybe that's where my crazy passion for problem-solving started. I got comfortable being uncomfortable. As a result, my customers mirror my confidence. That's why they were never concerned with any support situation—and they enjoyed watching me solve the issue.

TIP: I learned that confidence has a direct correlation to failure. When we shy away from failure and expect everything to be perfect and always go right, it can chip away at our self-confidence. When we accept and shift our mindset to the fact that failure is part of the learning process, it is incredible how much this builds our confidence. More importantly, this shifts our behaviours to how we react to these moments of failure in both our personal and professional lives.

CHAPTER 3

Why Projects?

Effective Communication. Conflict Resolution. Problem Solving and Leadership.

These are all valuable skills I've acquired... and can be applied in any industry of my choosing.

And this is exactly why people ask me: *Why projects?*

What is it that makes so many people, including myself, seek careers in Project Management... to deliver complex projects?

Well, the answer is simple: a great variety in your role day-to-day, opportunities available across most industries and this is where the demand is.

Now, bear with me, as I'm about to drop some statistics. Trust me, if you're considering a career in project management, knowing these numbers will be well worth it.

In 2017, the Project Management Institute Inc. (PMI) published a study that validated what I had chosen as my life's work.

They said demand for project managers is growing faster than the demand for workers in other occupations! And this is not an anomaly that is true only in one market. In fact, PMI studied seven project-oriented sectors in 11 countries... where they found consistently outstanding opportunities for project managers - both in terms of career growth and actual jobs.

And as if that's not enticing enough for anyone looking to start a career in project management...

This strong demand in growth is expected to continue on until 2027 at the very least! From 2017's figures, the project management labour market is expected to grow by 33 per cent. This means... if you're planning on joining the industry in the next few years… you could have your pick from about 22 million new jobs across 11 countries.

Pretty cool, isn't it?

Told you these stats are worth hearing about!

Oh, and one last crazy statistic from PMI: by 2027, employers would need about 88 million individuals in project management-oriented roles.

And it's not difficult to understand why.

See, over the last 15 years… we've gone through *at least* two major cycles of economic upheaval. First, we were hit with the Global Financial Crisis. Then, came the global pandemic. These left supply chains in shambles and threw economics and job prospects up in the air.

That's what I meant when I said there's bound to be massive demand for project managers for a long while.

I mean… who else would be better equipped to help organisations play catch up, manage, and deal with the ramifications of such widespread economic upheavals?

As such, being a project manager is a crazy good career option no matter what industry vertical you're considering working in.

But before we delve deeper into that, let's find out what a *project* actually is.

What is a Project?

I'm sure you've Googled the textbook (and rather boring) definition of what a project is.

A project is basically a temporary endeavour undertaken to create a unique product service… or result. Since it's temporary, there's always a definite beginning and end time for each project, unlike the routine activities organisations undertake to sustain their operations. After all, projects are completed once their specific goal or outcome is achieved.

Now, here's what all of that really means:

Businesses survive by having internal teams work on their day-to-day stuff. Those teams can't just drop the normal operational day-to-day stuff whenever the business needs to introduce something new... or if they want to enhance an existing service.

That's where project managers come in.

Instead of disrupting their day-to-day business operations, they bring in a dedicated team that will come in for a set period of time... to work on a set objective... in delivering a specific outcome. This team then delivers the enhancement or the new service. Once done, they will then hand the new system off to the internal team to manage as part of their day-to-day operations.

Of course, we don't just take on projects for other clients or organisations. We could also undertake personal and passion projects - but the same principles apply. We work on our personal projects for a specific period of time... with a specific outcome or result in mind... and we deem the project complete once that outcome or result is achieved.

Got it?

Now you know how projects work - in theory.

So, let's take things to the next level.

To show you how project management works in real life, let me tell you the story of my first-ever real project.

My First Project (And the 5 Biggest Mistakes I Made Along the Way)

I'm not going to lie.

My first-ever project could have gone *a lot* better. You know what they say - hindsight is always 20/20.

But while I can't go back in time to rectify some of the biggest mistakes I made during that first project... what I can do is share with you what those mistakes were... in hopes that you won't have to learn the same lessons I learned the hard way.

So, as I tell my story to uncover for you how project management works, we'll run through a bunch of useful lessons you can take with you... and use when the time comes.

Now, let's rewind right back to the beginning.

I started my apprenticeship as a Mechanical Aircraft Maintenance Ground Engineer with Qantas Airways Australia in 1990. I have a tonne of fond memories from that time.

I mean, who would have known that my love for all things mechanical and motor sports would eventually give me my first taste of project management?

See, I've been passionate about motor sports since I could remember.

If you're old enough to remember (and perhaps still watch) touring car racing... I was both inspired and excited by a local Australian driver who lived in Melbourne. His name is Allan Moffat and he drove a 1983 Mazda RX7 (back in the day). He's a four-time Bathurst winner and a legend in so many other respects.

In 1988, Allan Moffat and Gregg Hansford won the race at Sandown in their Eggenberger Motorsport-built Ford Sierra RS500. It was Moffat's 6th and final Sandown enduro win and was also Moffat's final race win as a driver in Australia. This spurred a deep passion in me – which was exacerbated by my days as an apprentice for Qantas Airways.

So, cue in for my first official project, which I started in 1990:

I decided to purchase and restore a 1970 Mazda RX2 Capella.

Mistake #1: Starting a project without fully understanding it.

Outside of just a vision of what the end result would look and feel like… I made this purchase without having a clear idea of any problem I was solving (or creating) with my choice.

I didn't even know if there were benefits to embarking on this journey! All I could think of was my dream, my vision, and my love for cars… and I let those things make my decisions for me.

As I rolled my RX2 out of the garage on an early Sunday morning, I did what I thought was the most logical next step - pull the car to pieces. I started to remove the interior of the car first… and methodically placed all the parts I was removing into storage containers.

In hindsight, the first thing I should have done was to consult car experts on the best approach to restoring my car. That would have given me a deeper understanding on what had to be done to make my vision come to life.

If I had made those consultations, I would have been better informed about the likelihood of finding rust in a place that put the structural integrity of my project car at risk. I would have known exactly what to do in that situation… and how much it would cost me. And I would have gained more insight into the availability of parts, seeing as the car was built in 1970.

Instead, I went right ahead with dismantling the vehicle. No budget allocation. Nothing to guide me through the steps I had to take to complete the project. Just the eagerness of a naïve project sponsor to get started as soon as possible.

My head was up in the clouds, but it shouldn't have been. Because while I was able to quickly roll out my first official project, it ended up becoming a three-year endeavour which didn't only challenge me financially... but also introduced me to all the complexities of a formal project. There I was, a young mechanical car enthusiast with zero experience in projects... learning the hard way that I needed more than my passion and vision to manage a project seamlessly.

So, here's my first tip for you:

Tip #1: Be clear about why you're doing what you're doing.

As Thomas Edison once said: **"Good fortune is what happens when opportunity meets with planning."**

Sometimes in life, fate would smile down on us, and it's as if everything just falls into place. But what I've learned from my first big mistake... was that you can't bank on luck alone. While opportunity is important, it will likely pass you by if you're not prepared enough for it.

When embarking on any project, it's important to have a full understanding of why you're doing it. And this reason has to be clear to you right from the ideation process and initiation phase. And when we talk about full understanding, we're not just talking about the end result. In fact, that's the easiest part.

All of us can have a grand vision of what we want to achieve.

The challenge is understanding what goals you need to set for yourself... in order to deliver that vision. That, and having a clear assessment of what benefits could be gained from undertaking such a project, if there are any. After that, sufficient thought must be put into the expected timeline and estimated budget needed to complete the project.

To be honest, I could have avoided a lot of unnecessary expenses - and heartache - had I gone through a structured planning process first before touching the car I bought. Or before buying it in the first place.

And that brings us to the second big mistake I made on my first-ever project:

Mistake #2: Starting a project without a plan

As analytical and methodical as I may have been, I never had a high-level or detailed plan in place before I started to dismantle the car.

So I had no plan, but was already well and truly committed to the car restoration. Six months in, I was already knee-deep in Project Execution. But that's when things started to get even more unhinged.

Not only were things progressing more slowly than expected. I also discovered that the budget needed to complete the work... was significantly more than I had envisioned. The discrepancy was too big to ignore!

Well, that's what I got for not having an overall budget cap in mind when I started the project - something I could have avoided if I had a structured plan for the whole thing! But as I've told you earlier... all I had was a dream. A vision of what I wanted the car to look like once I was done restoring it. I thought that as long as I had those things, no issue would be big enough to derail my vision.

That's where I was wrong.

The 20-year-old car started to give me financial and supply headaches. Many times, I had to pay a premium for the replacement parts I needed, as they weren't always readily available in Australia. As the requirements for the end result that I wanted started to materialise, so too did the time and money I needed to complete the project.

I hadn't even thought about what type of engine, fuel system, or suspension I was going to build for the car! These are things I could have determined much, much earlier into the restoration project. If only I had a structured plan to guide me... instead of me just "winging it."

Tip #2: Don't Plan to Fail

As Benjamin Franklin once said: **"If you fail to plan, you are planning to fail."**

Projects can be unpredictable. But 99% of the problems that could pop up can be avoided with better planning.

So, don't ever replicate the mistake I made.

In any project, planning should account for a significant portion of your timespan. In the planning stage, you should be able to:

- Identify all the key elements in delivering your project
- Document your technical requirements
- Validate your cost estimates
- Bring to the surface any potential constraints or risks associated with what you're planning to accomplish

Knowing all these things allows you to think about how you can manage such risks and complications… if they do come up.

See, it's not possible to take on a project that has zero risks. The best you can do is mitigate those risks by planning ahead. So, always create a detailed plan that can guide you through your project's journey… from start to finish.

Mistake #3: Not knowing the activities and the timeframe it takes to finish a project

18 months into my first-ever car restoration project, the car had been completely stripped and the body work had been completed. Despite starting without a full understanding of what I was about to do… or even a detailed plan to guide all my next steps, I still made considerable progress.

Once again - I was over the moon! I thought it wasn't so bad "winging it" after all. The car was truly starting to transform into the vision I had for it… and the core elements of the restoration had been done! I was finally getting my groove, and it seemed like the rest of the project could continue on without a problem.

Or so I thought. As it turns out, I was about to make even more mistakes that I sincerely hope you won't have to make yourself.

While I made progress with my restoration, I remember creating a shoe box to use as a filing system. I kept all my cost invoices in there. But as for the progress of the activities which had been completed at that point? I didn't have a quality or governance system for any of it! Yep, not even a shoe box...

I relied on my visual confirmation and my memory to track my progress - big mistake.

To this day, I can't tell you why I didn't keep a list of all the restoration activities I was working on. Perhaps, I was too confident of my understanding of the mechanical and technical constructs I was employing in my project... and to be fair, for quite some time, my knowledge of the subject matter sufficed to keep the project going. Against all odds, my personal understanding of what I was doing allowed me to maintain momentum and make me feel like I was in control.

Until it didn't.

I remember vividly how there were many times when I made decisions based on other people's recommendations. I also let my excitement get the better of me whenever I read about the latest trends in automotive restoration. Ironically, one of those automotive readings warned me about how the process of restoration can cause a shift in the restorer's mental state of mind... causing them to add more and more shiny bits to their project!

I didn't even realise I was already falling victim to this bad habit!

All of a sudden, I have deviated from the original plan I had in my head. Worse, I wasn't tracking my time and efforts anymore... not to mention the additional costs that the project kept incurring, thanks to the shiny bits I kept on adding to the original restoration project.

Looking back, I should have kept a better system for tracking the expenses and activities related to my project. My trusty old shoe box just didn't cut it. Having a better tracking system would have kept me in line, and I would have avoided so many unnecessary expenses. Who knows? Maybe I could have even wrapped up the project a lot faster!

Tip #3: Keep better track of your activities, expenses, and timeframe

Without a clear plan and list of activities related to your project… you will inevitably find yourself getting redirected away from your original objective. Be it because of stakeholders' opinions, a project sponsor's vision, or even the latest trends related to your project… you'd find it hard to resist picking up new requirements along the way. And while new requirements are not inherently bad, they could easily derail your project and ultimately add additional scope to what you're delivering, costing you more time and money overall.

So, my tip for you would be to respect the integrity of your original plan. Remember how I told you a vision was all I had when I embarked on my first-ever project? Well, had I stuck to a plan that supported this vision and not let anything else distract me from it, I would have successfully completed my project earlier.

If you want an efficient, productive, and smooth project execution with minimal issues… leverage the work done in your planning to keep you and your team focused on the planned activities. Track all your activities, expenses, and deadlines, so you can deliver the outcome needed, while keeping the project within budget, timeline, and at an accepted quality.

And though undoubtedly a mistake… this experience of losing track of my first-ever project taught me something that I would harness as part of my craft as a Project Delivery Professional. Dealing with such chaos sharpened my ability to identify small situations that can have a huge impact on my projects' outcome… even in ways that are unpredictable to the untrained eye.

Mistake #4: Falling victim to the creative process

Mistake #3 was all about getting distracted by external forces. On the other hand, Mistake #4 was falling victim to my own creative process.

How does that even happen, you ask?

Well, let's just say I let myself play Stanley Kubrick for too long.

Stanley Kubrick, one of the brightest minds in film directing, has been engaged in artistic projects his whole life. But the process by which he goes through it is quite unique. This is his approach to directing:

"I don't actually know what I want, but I'll know it when I see it."

So, he films stars like, say, Harvey Keitel walking through a doorway 80 times until he does it just right. He doesn't give a lot of directions, not even parameters on what it looks like to walk through a doorway the right way. He just instructs his actors to do the same thing enough times until he sees what he's looking for.

Now, if you're in an artistic field, and you have the right, supportive people around you... who can commit to a vision without even knowing what that vision is... then you might be able to get away with doing a Stanley Kubrick.

However, if you're dealing with a conventional project such as my car restoration, you're not going to have project managers willing to do something 80 times without any direction... in the hope that they're going to hit a bullseye for whatever your imagination might decide is the way to go.

It needs to be a lot more defined than that. You need a plan for how you're going to get from A to B, since your creative genius can't always pull you through without a structured plan to provide direction.

Trust me - I barely managed to pull through with all my crazy, creative ideas for my restoration project.

As you might have already noticed from my story so far, I'm a very ambitious guy. Sometimes, I'd get these grand visions of what I could do with my 1970 Mazda RX2 Capella, and I couldn't stop myself from trying to make those visions happen.

The problem was that I didn't stop to assess if those new visions were still in alignment with what I had originally planned, not to mention if I had enough money to see those new changes through. Again, I found myself extending the time needed to complete the car restoration project!

But not only that.

My rash, creative decisions also found a way to impact some of the other future projects I had in the pipeline at the time. Since my car restoration was costing way more than I originally thought it would... it ate into the funding I had allocated for a deposit to purchase an investment property.

Tip #4: Have a well-defined direction for your project

We can't all be Stanley Kubrick!

Never walk into a project blind. You must know exactly what your desired results are - and stick to it.

And how do you stick to the plan?

Of course, by monitoring and controlling the direction it's taking. This is a crucial element of project management... that's fundamental to keeping your project on track. By avoiding too many deviations from the original plan, you'll be able to ensure that your project remains within budget.

As an aspiring project management or delivery professional... I also urge you to get into the habit of thinking beyond your current project. This will help you avoid what happened to me where the onflow of my first project spilled over to future projects I had planned.

Part of this is of course learning to say no. And not just to other people. As a matter of fact, I've found in my experience that it's even harder to say no to yourself - or to your own 'creative' ideas.

But as Steve Jobs put it: **"[Success] comes from saying no to 1,000 things to make sure we don't get on the wrong track... or try to do too much. It's only by saying no that you can concentrate on the things that are really important."**

Now, before we move on to the fifth big mistake I made and the lesson I learned from it... let me just say one thing:

As the world's leading authority in project management, the Project Management Institute defines Project Management as the use of specific knowledge, skills, tools and techniques to deliver something of value to people.

From this perspective, I know I have broken most of the rules during my car restoration project and definitely did not have the skills, understanding, access to tools or techniques to manage and control the outcome of this personal project within a set timeframe or budget. That was what the first four mistakes were all about.

But still, I could say with confidence that the project was a success, as it delivered beyond the vision I had and provided me all the benefits I expected and have realised over the years since completing and closing the project in 1993.

Now, I'm not saying this to give you a free pass to make as many mistakes as I did. My point is that there are still ways to complete a project successfully... even though things may have started out rocky. The most important thing is that you learn how to move forward after every mishap. You've got to remain committed. There were many times I could have given up on my car restoration project when things didn't go as planned... but I remained committed. And that's how I was able to complete the project against all odds.

Still, despite knowing in my heart that the car restoration project was a success, there was one more mistake I wish I was able to avoid making:

Mistake #5: Not setting accurate objectives to help assess the project once done

I know I said the car restoration project eventually ended in a success...

But don't ask me if I finished the project on time or within budget - because I've never set a solid timeline or budget allocation for it! I just knew it took way longer and cost more than it should have... but I have no target metrics to compare my actual results to!

Also, don't ask me if I fully realised the benefits of the project outcome as originally thought - because again, I didn't even think about any potential benefits when I started the project!

Not having a plan, an allocated time frame, or a budget definitely made for a bumpy, unpredictable ride. I made it to the end, but it would have been really nice to have a matrix I could have used to assess the project once it was completed.

Tip #5: Use a Requirements Traceability Matrix (RTM)

When we complete the final delivery of our projects and progress to Project Closure, the next best thing to do is to carry out an assessment of the project. It's always good to know what went well, and what could have been improved - since you can use all this knowledge to make your next projects go even better.

It is at this juncture that you'd realise the things you missed during the Project Planning and Execution which can sometimes make it difficult for you to validate what has been delivered... and even to confirm if the benefits can be realised.

That's why I encourage the use of an RTM - or a Requirements Traceability Matrix. This is a working document which you could (and should) reference and update throughout the entire project delivery lifecycle.

The first thing your RTM should contain are the project requirements. And apart from aligning the requirements to the list of activities you're supposed to undertake... your RTM should also include tests and acceptance criteria for post implementation validation. In other words, you should have specific criteria to validate that a task is considered successfully completed.

Doing this would help you with your PIR - or Project Implementation Review. This is where you sit down and review the project you have completed. Discuss with your team what you think went well and what didn't go so well.

Having this assessment is another fundamental element that Project Delivery Professionals should embrace. It's part of having this continuous improvement mindset. As mentioned earlier, all learnings - whether good or bad - can be used as ammunition to really hit the bullseye on your next projects.

As a project team, being able to come together and encourage open discussions based on a role-based perspective for the project is invaluable not only for the insights you'll gain but also in providing a forum for the team to share and be heard as individuals.

Reviewing and validating the expected outcomes of the project as per your RTM and being able to review any missed targets will also drive discussions and allow everyone to make recommendations for improvement as part of project closure.

And speaking of closure, I've told you several things you likely wouldn't have asked me about my first project.

Now, let me tell you about one question you can ask and I'd gladly answer:

Was I happy with the end-result, despite the very rocky road I took to get there?

Most definitely.

I mean, look at the end result in question:

To this day, this sweet ride is still with me.

I know I only promised five lessons… but here's the sixth one, which I also touched upon earlier:

Even when you mess up and make one, three, or five big mistakes in project management… things can still work out in your favour… and things will turn out okay.

So, how much more enjoyment could you have and success in delivering projects if you *didn't* make any big mistakes… and if you planned your project properly from beginning to end?

You could be unstoppable.

Why Project Management Might Be Good for You

As you've learned from my story, I started my Project Management experience as a Car Enthusiast... and developed it further as part of my journey with Qantas Airways as a Ground Engineer.

I leveraged my knowledge in Aircraft Maintenance processes and got involved in working with Engineering Systems projects... and then eventually transitioned formally into the Information Technology Domain.

I then managed to truly apply my learnings and experience... and found my "love" for projects when I set up my own IT Support & Consulting Business. There, running projects was infused into my way of thinking and it also ticked so many boxes for me personally.

So now, I want to share with you why I think Project Management might also be a good choice for you:

1. **No two days are the same**.

If you enjoy variety and challenges in life... you'll be glad to know that no two projects are ever the same. Even if you're delivering the same service... product... or perceived outcome, each project will be unique in its own way. Personally, I always seek to break the monotony of doing the same things day in and day out, which is why I never warmed up to the idea of having an office or a desk job. If you're the same way, then rest assured that project management and delivery offers a lot of variety and challenges. You'd be forced to grow, innovate, and do things you've never done before - a total treat, as far as I'm concerned!

2. **Leading Edge Technology and Change Agent**

Delivering projects is all about leading change. I see Project Delivery Professionals as change agents who not only have the benefit of delivering leading edge tech or greenfield products/services... but also being at the forefront of transforming organisations. The level of impact you'd be making as a professional in this industry is simply unparalleled. If you're like me, and would grab any opportunity to lead change, make an impact, and also play with new tech before everyone else... then this career path is definitely for you.

3. **Industry Agnostic**

Where an aircraft engineer is trained as a specialist to work specifically on aircraft... a Project Delivery Professional acquires a set of skills... which they can apply even as they transfer across other industries. See, Project Management principles are similar wherever you go. You just have to add a bit of knowledge around the particular industry or domain you're developing next.

I have personally worked across a multitude of industry types as a Project Manager. Again, I love this because it satisfies my need for job diversity... which keeps me interested and motivated in what I do.

4. **Personal Development**

If I were to list the multitude of opportunities that could provide you with personal development as a Project Delivery Professional... you would be astounded.

Not only can you continue to develop professionally with the ever-evolving project management frameworks and methodologies (i.e., certifications)... but you will also encounter many opportunities to discover who you are... while also applying and practising the many soft skills you'd be acquiring as a Project Delivery Professional. Personally, there is a growth aspect to why I chose Project Management. So, if you've always wanted to focus on personal development and growth, you're on the right path.

5. **Communication**

Here's something I discovered and have proven to be 100% accurate:

Project Management will give you a brand-new perspective on communication. See, communication is the lifeblood of project management. Without communication, it would be near-impossible to drive project success.

This means every day you work in project management is an opportunity to refine, develop and master your communication skills - both verbal and non-verbal.

From when I started... it's amazing how I have developed personally in this area. I have gained the ability to understand what my team members are saying - and what they're not saying. This is a very POWERFUL element, not just for project delivery professionals, but for anyone! When mastered, communication skills can transform the results you see in how you deliver projects... also how you manage your teams and other aspects of your life.

6. **Leadership**

In case I haven't made it clear just yet... Project Delivery Professionals are **Leaders**.

From the time you take on your first project, you'd start to see yourself as such. That means you'll be embracing what it truly means to be a leader.

See, leadership is not just about managing people. Surely, you've come across one manager in your life that stands out above the rest. I'm pretty sure you're drawn towards and are influenced by this manager... and perhaps you can't even explain *why*. And that's because good leadership is difficult to encapsulate in words. It might seem like an abstract, inherent characteristic that only a few people have... but believe me when I say:

Leadership is something you can learn and develop as part of Project Management. We can't underestimate the power of leadership in projects. The multitude of challenges and situations you will face... will have you testing and refining those leadership skills day in and day out.

7. **Increase Your Value**

As I grew and developed myself through professional experience and personal development... I have been able to increase my value in the marketplace.

It's not even just about collecting Project Management certifications. See, when you develop yourself and start to provide more than what your CV reflects... that's when the magic starts to happen. And I sincerely believe that projects provide this opportunity for growth... beyond what you can document on paper.

As Jim Rohn puts it: *"**Learn to work harder on yourself than you do on your job. If you work hard on your job you can make a living, but if you work hard on yourself you'll make a fortune.**"*

This is why I recommend Project Management and Delivery to anyone who seeks to increase their value as a person... and as a professional.

8. Career Prospects

For many careers, the long-term career roadmaps or pathways are limited. However, the same is not true in Project Management. From being a Project Coordinator to a Portfolio or PMO Manager role, the various positions across many industries that you can work in... are endless. Depending on your preference, you even have a choice between project management with a Business Focus... or a Specialist Product/Service focus!

I embrace and enjoy this flexibility in career direction when it comes to projects, because it means my destiny will be determined by ME... and I can make the best choices based on the area of interest or learning I want... or even based on where I am at in my own personal life.

9. Unlimited Potential for FUN

Finally, I see projects as a structured way to embrace change and bring people together for a common cause - which is to drive the outcome you need to deliver. I always consider project team members as a "temporary" family who stick together no matter what... and really getting to know each other on the job.

Yes, projects and project management will never be your typical 9-5 job, where you come home as the clock strikes 5 and you relax, go to bed, and then do it all again in the morning.

Here, you might have a 2am call with an offshore team... and then have to show up for an after-hours implementation. There are many ups and downs in this line of work, but it does not mean we cannot have fun and enjoy the opportunities that some of the challenges bring us.

After all, FUN is at the core of my relationship with my teams!

Now, I can't help but get excited wondering what your first - or next - project will be. I can't wait to see how the Project Management industry will evolve over the next 10-20 years... and if you will be one of the pioneers who inspire and motivate newcomers to the industry... by living to tell *your* tale. Just the way I'm doing now!

If you're excited about these things, too, then keep reading!

Because in the next chapter, we'll talk about some refinements you could introduce into your habits... to better prepare you for a career in Project Management.

What I Learned From Running an IT Consulting Business: RISK, REWARDS, & RESULTS

As I developed the business model for my IT Consulting Business, I was able to dial in my entrepreneurial spirit... to understand the marketplace and my customers better.

Soon, I was able to expand the services I had to offer. I then became the Principal Project & IT Consultant for a business with a 6-staff team! Needless to say, the stakes were higher. And so too were the risks.

With this comes my next hard-earned lesson - it's about RISK, REWARDS, & RESULTS.

Since I was now working to deliver six-figure solutions to my clients, the element of risk and exposure began to materialise. I was no longer just getting involved in things that I knew! As a Systems Integrator, I also needed to rally my team behind systems and platforms... of which we were not experts. We were striving to learn as fast as we could, knowing full well that we were also working with vendors who were dependent on us to succeed.

See, to fully enjoy the highest level of REWARDS and RESULTS possible in Project Management, we definitely had to take on some RISK and adventure along the way. You can't always stay within your comfort zone. It will always be important to seek opportunities for more profit... by bringing your products and services to new markets.

Here's a wonderful quote by American minister and author Norman Vincent Peale... who is best known for his work on positive thinking:

"Shoot for the moon. Even if you miss, you'll land among the stars."

I 100% agree. As you've learned from my first-ever project, I'm a firm believer that we can achieve other great things while trying to do one great thing... even if you don't achieve your original goal.

The important thing is to not shy away from risks. Because only by taking on those risks will you be able to get great results - and be rewarded for it.

TIP: I learned that a life of complacency is not a life well-lived. I personally discovered how doing and achieving things that are easy - doesn't always drive the best results for me. Instead, it is in striving for things that are bigger than us, and adding that magical element of risk... where we could get the best return for our efforts - both in results and rewards.

As a Project Delivery Professional or Corporate Leader... you'd sometimes find that it's easy to stay in our comfort zone and not stretch ourselves beyond what we're sure we're capable of.

But there's no going around this. Eventually, you will have to run your first million-dollar project. And it might be a bumpy ride, what with all the risks you have to take... but once you make it through, you will realise you have learnt so much and grown from the experience... while building your confidence and then ultimately increasing your value in the market through the experience you have gained. That's when you know the RISKS you took… have delivered great RESULTS & REWARDS for you.

CHAPTER 4

Amplifying Strengths and Mitigating Weaknesses

3:30 a.m.

The alarm clock goes off.

Just like clockwork, my day starts.

I quickly get my brain into gear and start planning all the things I need to get done today. My brain is awash with so many project tasks. *Got to do this, got to do that, and then that other thing...*

I don't even have time for breakfast.

Just like I didn't have time for breakfast yesterday, and the day before that, and the week before that.

I grab my gear, make sure I haven't forgotten anything, jump in the car, and head straight to the office. For the whole car ride, my mind races.

How am I going to get through the day?

What's going to happen today?

What can go wrong this time that I might potentially pre-empt?

The rest of my day is full of energy. Lots of things going on. Interacting with customers... dealing with technical challenges with the team... putting out small fires here and there...

And before I know it, I miss lunch time. Yep, that's my second missed meal of the day. No worries - it's all part of the routine. This is usually what happens when I'm out in the trenches doing what I know best: keeping customers of my IT Support & Consulting business happy.

Sometimes, with all good intentions, I'd quickly make a sandwich to eat on the drive from one client site to another. Then, I'd finish meeting with the five clients we were juggling... and only then do I remember the now-pitiful sandwich sitting on my passenger seat - already too warm from sitting in the sun and too soggy to be enjoyed.

Day after day, I find myself absorbed and consumed by the projects and activities my team and I needed to get through. And so I started to build these habits and behaviours - including missing most of my lunchtime meals. I think to myself: my body's going to punish me for this. But I guess it's just amazing how our bodies can adapt. I never really got punished for all those missed meals. My body just... got used to it.

And so did my family and friends.

Many times like today, as I go through the motions of what I have to do, sometimes never actually knowing what time of day it was... how many hours had gone by since I even started my day... and whether or not the sun had already set. I look down at my watch for the first time... and realise it was way too late and that I'm already missing a get-together my wife organised with some of our friends.

So I jump back in my car (soggy sandwich still on the passenger seat) and head home. My wife welcomes me with a frown for missing most of the dinner she'd organised months ago. But she doesn't give me a lot of trouble about it. I guess she was hoping for a miracle (a.k.a. me actually keeping track of my time and being punctual for once)... but deep down I know she's used to it.

It was interesting how life seemed to adjust accordingly to my crazy routine. Me being late to functions or outings was already considered the norm for my friends and family... I just knew if I somehow made it on time to one of our gatherings, they'd be left having to pick their jaws up from the floor.

Still, I know there's one question that lingers on everybody's mind whenever I walk in the door in a rush, apologising profusely for being late once more. That question is:

Is he doing this on purpose?

42

And the answer is *no*.

One day, I was just settling into a new routine which involved delivering projects for five different clients. The next day, here I am, missing meals and personal commitments... the mind and body, always being rushed from one place to another.

All of this seemed to have started to happen on autopilot.

Worse, I thought I was doing everything in my life consciously.

And sure, I may have been making some decisions around small, work-related things... but in general, my life was now starting to run on semi-autopilot.

The question is: Is this a good thing? Or is it a bad thing?

Well, sometimes, it can be a sign of a really good thing... because it can indicate that you've reached a state of flow. Other times, it can be really, really, really bad. Because it means we've become so tunnel visioned, that we're no longer able to take on extra stimuli... which prevents us from arriving at better solutions to more complex problems.

And where our ability to adapt is limited, we tend to stop evolving. And that stops higher thought processes from giving us something that we might really need in order to take our lives to the next level.

Case in point:

Health and wellness have always been important to me. All my life, personal care has been something I take in high regard. Ever since my life started to run on autopilot though, I now find myself making excuses... like not having the energy to go to the gym or out for my (supposedly) daily run. Without realising it, I've shifted my priorities to working longer hours, and spending most of my mental energies in managing our complex projects. Slowly over time, I began to lose the energy and vitality I'd always had for life.

Another real passion of mine is personal development — be it daily learnings which can be used for either professional and/or personal growth. Enriching my mind was something I enjoyed immensely, keeping me on the edge of my seat with life. But hey — I already told you about how often I've been missing meals, right? And how little time I got to spend with my family since life began running on autopilot. Suffice it to say, anything to do with my personal or professional development was also thrown out the window, too.

It's interesting how we go through life thinking that we are in total control of everything that we do. It's amazing to think that although we wake up and open our eyes each day... we still sometimes walk through life BLINDLY.

Just like what happened with me, you form brand new habits without even realising it.

From the outside, people probably think I was a highly intentional and highly organised person who handles everything extremely well. But on the inside, I wasn't doing a lot of thinking. I wasn't prioritising things intentionally. I wasn't organised.

* * *

3:30 a.m.

The alarm clock goes off.

Just like clockwork, I wake up.

But today, I can't get out of bed.

I'm absolutely on the verge of burning out.

I have no idea what I'm supposed to do, and it's been so long since I've given these things a proper, genuine thought.

For quite a while, my routine got me through the day on autopilot. But now, I'm stuck. I've realised that I need to think beyond just working with projects and clients.

I realise I want to be more conscious about how I was living life. No more of this autopilot stuff! I want to eat better, adopt better habits, and really think about what behaviours are serving me... and which ones are not serving me that I need to change about myself.

I want to be in control again.

For a long time, I struggled. Yet I worked through things and persevered relentlessly... thinking that being busy running my business round-the-clock was a wonderful problem to have. Thinking that missing meals was proof that I was doing something meaningful. Thinking that showing up late for functions with my family and friends was acceptable... because I thought I was doing the right thing by working extremely hard.

Ironically, project delivery professionals like myself are really methodical and logical people. We love working on large, complex projects by default. But for so long, I failed to apply this same methodical and logical approach to my personal life.

It was like having "highway hypnosis" for years.

Ever get in a car... drive somewhere... and actually make it to your destination safe and sound... and yet have no recollection of the entire trip? That's what highway hypnosis is. You make all the right turns, you make every decision that gets you somewhere... but you're not really conscious while you're doing them.

This happens a lot when drivers are too tired to actually mind the journey.

And with everything I was trying to juggle in my life and business... it totally makes sense.

Thank goodness I had this realisation.

Thank goodness I woke up to a very important turning point in my life.

Thank goodness I decided to write things down... and audit my life for the first time in a really long while. I found that the easiest and simplest way to do that audit was to write it all out. Just like an accountant would. I recognised this was not the most exciting process - but it's important work.

Because it's what I needed to do if I wanted to drive my life with both eyes open.

Harnessing Your Potential for Better Outcomes

I'm sure you know what everyone's favourite part of riding on an aeroplane is.

The safety demonstration, of course!

You know, it's when they tell you that in case of an impending crash... you've got to put your head between your knees. Nothing like a nice mental image of you plummeting at 900 kilometres an hour just before you take to the skies, no?

But seriously... there is one thing they tell you during these demonstrations that's really important. They say that if an emergency does happen... and the oxygen masks drop from the ceiling... you're supposed to put on your own mask first.

They reiterate this a couple of times: before helping other passengers put their masks on, put yours on first.

Because if you insist on helping other people before you mask yourself up... you're going to have to hold your breath for a good while. And while you scramble to get back to your mask in time, it may be too late and you could start to turn blue yourself.

As you can tell from the story I told you earlier... I've been in that situation where I was already turning blue.

And I'm not alone. Despite constant reminders from flight attendants and other professionals to take care of one's self first, when push comes to shove... a vast majority of people still spend 99% of their lives looking after other people and their projects... *before* taking care of themselves first as the REAL priority.

Perhaps you've even felt the exact same thing... especially if you've worked on a whole lot of large, complex and stressful projects.

So, let me reiterate what every flight attendant hopes you'd have remembered by now: Put on your own oxygen mask first. Work out where you're spending most of your energy on, and realign your priorities with the outcomes you want to achieve in your life. See, by serving yourself first, you'll be in a better position to serve other people, like your clients.

That's exactly what I did when I finally woke up with a realisation that my life needed reviewing and auditing. In the interest of saving and serving myself first... I worked out where I was doing well in my life... and where I was falling short, or even failing. And by leveraging my strengths and mitigating my weaknesses... I was able to harness my own true potential to see the results I wanted in my life... and in my business as well.

So, where exactly should you start when auditing your life for better outcomes?

Well, I do believe our behaviours, daily routines and habits set the stage for everything we do in life... so why not start there?

As project delivery professionals, corporate leaders, and employees... it's important for us to have a deep understanding of the behaviours we exhibit daily... especially when we are in stressful situations.

A very simple technique you can use is to simply write down in a journal or notepad what you're feeling or thinking during these stressful situations... and how those emotions and thoughts manifest into the actions and behaviours we exhibit during those moments.

See, writing things down helps you become more conscious and allows you to acknowledge your own feelings and thought processes... which eventually sets the tone for how you manage your life.

Creating and building this habit of recognising your own thoughts, feelings, and behaviour (self-awareness)... will force you to be more present in every moment. It also allows you to understand your internal thought processes more intently.

For instance, if you find out that you sometimes make rash decisions when you're feeling upset... then you can decide not to make any decisions until you're in a fully calm and logical state!

Trust me, the simple act of writing down what's happening within you... can help you make better sense of what's happening around you that you may not even be conscious of.

For example...

It wasn't until I started to write down the things that were happening to me... that I started to:

- Become deeply aware of the disappointment I was creating for my family, instead of giving myself a free pass because "all I was doing was working hard!"
- Acknowledge the way that I had let my health go.
- Determine the habits that I had formed which were not serving me, like missing meals or only eating fast food... instead of making the effort to pack a healthy lunch.
- Realise that I had convinced myself that what I was doing was way more important than resting... and that I had no choice but to keep working round-the-clock... instead of stopping once in a while to recharge my mind, body, and soul.

But here's the most painful realisation I had as part of my self-assessment project:

I realised I had actually really given up on myself.

I had given up on learning... which was the catalyst for my growth both personally and professionally. I came to the regretful conclusion that I had been too consumed in the things that were causing me the most pain in my life... and was transforming my world in a way that did not serve me, to say the least.

As painful as this was, having all these realisations helped me do one thing:

It made me capable of changing things... so I could start living life in a way that served me. By being more conscious of where I was doing great, and where I was letting things fall through the cracks... I managed to pull myself back into line.

See, once you start to get into the habit of auditing your life and keeping tabs on yourself... the conscious awakening which happens within you is incredible!

When you make the decision to become more conscious of your daily routine and habits... and start to really look at how those habits or rituals are serving you... you'll find that many other opportunities will open up before your eyes.

Way too many of us find ourselves stuck... not realising that the reason we are where we are is a combination of how we think... how we behave... and how we bring consciousness to the things we are so used to doing unconsciously.

So, I want you to take a really honest look at where you currently are. What are the thoughts, emotions, behaviours, and habits that have brought you here? And what are the thoughts, emotions, behaviours, and habits that are stopping you from taking a step further... into where you actually want to be?

Go deep and honestly look at what you're good at... and which areas you need to focus on so you can excel. By doing this, you can start to improve on what you're already good at... and then manage what you're not so good at.

This way, you can really push and achieve all the things you've always wanted to achieve.

And if you need a bit more help with this admittedly complicated process of understanding one's self... let's take a page out of the book of one of my personal development coaches - Scott Harris from Authentic Results / Ultimate Coach.

One of the best concepts I learnt from him was called Feather Brick Truck. I bet this would be immensely helpful in unleashing your full potential, too... so let me explain more about what the Feather Brick Truck is.

The Feather Brick Truck Concept

Feather Brick Truck is a three-stage concept you can use to get to know yourself better.

Let's start with the FEATHER Stage.

Both success and failure leave clues - we just have to be better at spotting them.

See, sometimes the situations we find ourselves in every day... have a way of letting us know whether we're on the right path... or if we might need to shift gears... change directions... or make some decisions.

That's what the FEATHER concept is all about — recognising that little "tickle"... that little inkling... that recurring (and sometimes nagging) feeling... which is trying to let you know that something's not right. Chances are, you've had times where you *know* something's wrong, although you can't really put your finger on what made you think that way. You just feel it. It's not something that will stop us in our tracks, but it's basically something that will be annoying and just doesn't feel right. Yet most of us will push through that feeling as we are so used to ignoring this stage by default. You feel it in your gut. You feel it in your body.

Unfortunately, when we find ourselves in these situations, that little tickle is very EASY to ignore. We even convince ourselves into thinking that perhaps... we're just being paranoid!

50

In effect, we don't let that little ticklish FEATHER stop us in our tracks. Although we already have an inkling that something doesn't feel right, we tend to brush it off as normal or nothing to worry about.

In Project Management, the feather tickles when we fail to set boundaries in how we operate. That's when we find ourselves committing to longer and longer hours at work.

At first, it's just a few nights a week of extra time. We get the feeling we shouldn't be doing it, but we ignore that feeling. Until we wake up one day having worked a whole lot of extra time for a whole year. And only then do we realise that we should have listened to that annoying, nagging feeling we got when we first started working late. You know, the little feather that tickled us and said:

Heyyyy... hate to bother you... but I reallllly don't think you should be working this late.

For many of us, these "feather" moments are something that we don't even realise is at play. So, the next time you feel a ticklish feather telling you something doesn't feel right, assess whatever you're doing and start asking yourself:

Does this have a negative impact on my well-being in the short term?

Does it have any other impact in my world... perhaps to my family and friends... or the way I'm living other aspects of my life?

And if so, how can I possibly do better?

Because I assure you... if you don't start asking these questions... and if you continue ignoring that FEATHER...

You'll eventually find yourself faced with the next phase:

The BRICK Stage.

Spoiler alert: if the feather stage was a gentle reminder of what you could be doing wrong... the BRICK stage is, well, a lot less gentle.

See, when we end up in the brick stage... that means we ignored all the feather moments and proceeded to do the exact thing we were warned by the feather not to.

And so now, we may have to pay the price.

When we end up in the brick stage, we find ourselves facing the same things which presented themselves during the feather stage, except that time has passed. The fact that time has passed means we have endured multiple feathers over an extended period of time, so those little insignificant feather moments that we have been putting up with for so long now are going to potentially start to have a direct or indirect psychological or physiological impact on our being.

It won't be pretty.

Let's go back to our example earlier about spending more time in the office than you're supposed to. Assuming you've ignored the feather, you may now find yourself working 16-hour workdays… every day for YEARS. Burning the candle at both ends now becomes your NORM.

Say, you're working on a large complex project… and it's taking a significant amount of your focus and time to drive the results and outcomes needed.

Here comes the impact we were talking about earlier.

Your body now starts to react to not getting a lot of sleep… along with the fact that you've stopped exercising because you don't have time. So, you're now starting to feel it's getting harder to get up in the morning. And even going to bed at night proves to be a challenge… as you find your head is constantly full of thoughts. You struggle to get the quality sleep that you need within the small window of time that you do have… and it starts to affect your overall functionality in the morning.

Oh, and those small moments where your family expressed their concerns about you missing functions, events, and even simple dinners with the family? You realise they're not doing it anymore. Not because you've been doing better at showing up… but because they've stopped expecting as much from you. Now your work is having a negative impact on the synergies and meaningful connections you have in your life.

So, you wake up one morning and instead of immediately jumping out of the bed like you always do… you find yourself with a throbbing headache and a body that refuses to move an inch.

That only means one thing:

You've finally been hit by the BRICK.

And while it's possible to ignore the gentle tickling of the FEATHER... believe me when I say getting hit by a brick this time... will definitely stop you in your tracks temporarily. Maybe not forever... but you'd need to at least take a day... to recover from getting hit by a brick.

Sure, it wouldn't kill you, but the Brick phase is designed to inflict some pain and slow you down. It is designed to make you pay ATTENTION.

And there lies the beauty of the Brick. Now, you get a physical sign that will make you more aware of the path you're on... giving you a fair chance to assess your daily routines and habits... and make some changes in it.

But you've got to take it seriously. And you've got to make those changes soon.

Because if you don't... well, you'd have to move on to the final stage in the process:

The TRUCK stage.

If you ever reach this stage where you need to get hit by a truck to get you to pay attention and change directions... it means you were too stubborn and ignored both warnings from the FEATHER and the BRICK.

That means... although you've now found yourself in several situations where you were knocked flat on your back... unable to get out of bed or properly function mentally... you continued on along the path of destruction you were in.

You refused to reassess and change the things you are doing.

So here comes the TRUCK (which has been parked on the side of the road all this time watching you)... and it's headed right for you.

This now becomes the final stage which could transform your world forever... but obviously not in a positive way... and not for any of the right reasons!

You've been given sufficient warnings in the last two stages to shift and change your behaviour... but you did not waiver. So, the universe has no choice but to send you its least gentle warning yet... and you end up being hit - and run over - by what feels like a truck.

Now, while you may be able to recover from getting hit by a brick after just a day or two of resting... the same is not true when you get hit by a truck. This time, even though you might still be able to recover... you'd be left with long-term scars and damage, sometimes both mentally and physically.

Well, if that's what it takes to disrupt your personal and professional life so you can finally do better... that's sometimes what you have to endure.

The physiological and psychological impacts now become difficult to ignore by you.

You will fall sick; your body will react, and you will struggle to maintain a normal, functional existence.

Many leaders in Project Management and even those that work in the corporate world tolerate undue stress that doesn't serve them... but it only overwhelms and takes them to a point on the brink of potential BURNOUT sometimes.

If this sounds like you, beware! It might only be a matter of time before that truck pulls out from the curb and heads straight for you. You now have a very small window of opportunity to possibly change things around in your life... and hopefully derail that truck before it hits you.

If it does hit you, however... all hope is not lost.

There is still a chance for recovery.

How long it will take is a different question altogether.

The only determining factor to how quickly you can recover from the truck stage is how far you've pushed yourself within both the feather and brick stage. Were you able to change things, even a little?

And right now, as we speak, what with the negative circumstances you still find yourself in ... do you have the courage to change things?

Now, let's address the elephant in the room.

I know we've said it's possible for a truck to NOT stop you in your tracks. Yet, you'd be left in the recovery stage for an extended period of time... but I know that for some people, this is still not a guarantee that they'd do things differently next time.

See, some people would still be too stubborn... and will still try to persevere and continue in the same way they know. I hope you're not one of those people. Because ultimately... without a change in what you are doing, any attempts at recovery will likely be foiled. Before you know it, here comes that truck again.

You will be knocked off your feet once again for a significant amount of time... at which point it may just depend on your level of resilience and both your physiological and psychological state to determine how quickly you get back to your life.

It's really important at this point to understand that even though the concept of the Feather, Brick & Truck is simple enough to understand... applying it in practice is a bigger challenge. That's why you have to make the extra effort to identify these three warning signs.

Remember: there's only so many times a person can be knocked out and run over by a truck... before they lose any and all hope for recovery.

So, while you've still got time... save yourself.

Know Yourself

Only by knowing yourself can you effectively save yourself.

I know this, because I've been tickled by a feather or too in my time. I've taken a brick to the face many times. And when I still wouldn't change, I got run over by a truck or two. But I didn't let any of those things happen again. This habit of conscious decision-making and self-awareness is now part of my being.

Even though I started out on this journey with highway hypnosis, I've learned how to live a more conscious existence. I am now well aware of all the things that I SAY... the things that I DO... and even the things I don't say or do.

And it all started with getting to know myself better. By placing my own personal life on audit, so I could apply my project management skills and take better control of my life.

So, ultimately, your first mission (as was mine)... is to start to become more conscious about your behaviours... feelings... and thoughts. Especially in tough situations where your rational brain is challenged to come up with the best solution to the problem at hand. This way, you can uncover what your strengths and weaknesses are.

And once you learn how to enhance your strengths and mitigate your weaknesses... you can finally work towards unleashing your full potential... and achieving the outcomes you've been working so hard all this time to achieve.

You know... just like you help other people achieve theirs.

Remember the flight announcements. You've got to put your own oxygen mask on first... before you even think about saving and serving other people.

And also remember what Les Brown said: **"You are the only real obstacle in your path to a fulfilling life."**

Don't wait for that proverbial truck to hit you. As soon as you feel that feather tickling something within you... don't just stand there in the same place. Go out there and redirect your life. That's the best way to know yourself, save yourself, and serve yourself.

What I Learned From Running an IT Consulting Business: INDEPENDENCE

The dynamics of running a business and leveraging my ideas as a true entrepreneur in the marketplace... has forced me to pave my own path at times... walking in a direction that has never been walked on before. To this day, I know many decisions I make as an entrepreneur focus on going against the grain.

That's why I consider INDEPENDENCE as one of the most significant lessons I've learned while running my IT & Consulting Business.

In business, it's much easier to walk where others have walked. That means completely modelling our business from other successful businesses... which already have systems that have been proven to work.

But I must say... nothing compares with the fulfilment of doing things your own way.

For many years, I modelled my business after other successful businesses around me. But there were also a lot of elements which I did not necessarily agree with... and intentionally did not adopt into my own model.

See, I've always loved and still today embrace the concept of a unique selling proposition (USP). It's the one thing that sets your business apart from the competition. It's a specific benefit that makes your business stand out... when compared to other businesses in the market.

So, as our USP... I leveraged part of our company mission statement which was to **"Make Customer Service Matter."**

And boy, what an impact this made to our customer base and the endorsed referrals we received for our services.

Project Delivery Professionals & Corporate Leaders, too often forget that we too have a USP. As such, many of us are driven into blending in with the marketplace, talking the same talk, getting the same qualifications, and even writing up our professional resumes in the same format.

And this only leads to all of us also getting the same results.

We forget about ALL the individual attributes and experiences that make us unique.

TIP: When you stand independently… you start to make sense of the world around you based on your own personal observations and experiences… rather than just going along with the thoughts of others.

And that's how you strike gold.

As a Success Coach and founder of Project Managers Movement I always encourage people to digest my advice, stories, and perspectives. But I also tell them to independently dissect, review, and understand those things… so they can create their own version of the ideas that are applicable to them.

I do not believe in a one-size-fits-all approach. Which is why I practise my independent thinking skills daily. I believe great leaders are independent thinkers who trust their own ability to make judgments.

I mean, just take a look at the founder of three disruptive companies: SpaceX, PayPal and Tesla.

Elon Musk is not just another innovator/entrepreneur. He's also a disruptor and a game-changer in the multitude of industries he's in. While most people are discouraged by criticism and negative feedback to their ideas (which is why many people seek to avoid criticism and negativity by always going along with the popular opinion)... Elon listens intently to any negative feedback so that he can identify blind spots in his own ideas.

Now, imagine what ideas you could unlock from within... when you consciously trust yourself and choose to formulate your own opinion and independent perspective.

I bet they'd be great ideas.

And I can't wait to see those ideas turn into action.

CHAPTER 5

Build a Support Network

Project management is an exciting career.

If you're lucky, when you're delivering projects, you might get to put Murphy's Law to shame.

A few years back, my team and I were put in that exact situation. We had a cyber security project where we had to upgrade a company's firewalls. As is required for projects of this magnitude... our team spent months putting together a plan to upgrade those firewalls without disrupting the clients' corporate network.

After all, the client had asked us if there was a way to do the necessary upgrades... without disrupting their operations.

And we said possibly.

So, we spent the next month planning and making sure we had the right technical team for the job. We had technical network engineers... security specialists... and even vendor consultants. Everyone was on site, ready to do their part in the implementation.

We were to start the firewall upgrades at 6 p.m. And so as the clock counts down to showtime, I stand back and let the team work their magic. The technical lead took over, and he started to direct the team across the multiple implementation steps we prepared to deliver the outcome we were being paid to deliver.

The team completed all the pre-checks to make sure that all production network traffic is flowing as it should.

We got the green light.

So far, so good.

And then, we get to the most critical part of the implementation. It's where we flip the traffic between the old firewalls and the newly installed ones.

That's when things started to go wrong.

All of a sudden, the security specialist says they're not seeing any traffic flowing through the new firewalls. It's like an electric shock runs through the entire team as they all turn to their computers to see what's happening.

What have we missed?

What did we do wrong?

What can we do to fix this?

What is the impact on operations?

And the technical lead calls it: internet traffic was not flowing.

Panic ensues.

Yep, it's very rare that the internet breaks like this. Without having to talk to one another, the entire team knew that either someone did something wrong or we missed something in the environment that potentially is causing this behaviour which we did not expect.

At that point, nobody knew.

All we know is that a whole lot of technical people were staring very, very intently at their computer screens… hoping that someone else was going to find the problem. Radio silence is never a good sign when the team is faced with a problem to solve.

That's when I, the project manager, emerged from the shadows. If everything had gone well, I could have just sat back, letting the team execute the work we spent months planning.

But everything did not go well.

That's when I make that call to the IT Service Desk, advising them of the situation that was playing out.

I ask the dreaded question.

Have you received any calls from any part of the business advising that they're impacted by what's happening at the moment?

A pregnant, three-second pause.

That's all it took for the other person to answer. But to me, it felt like an eternity.

Finally, I got a response.

Yes, we've had a few calls saying people are not able to access their external systems.

The adrenaline kicks in. I drop the phone and get back to my team and swiftly tell them:

We're in trouble. The implementation issue is now affecting production. We need to assess this really quickly.

Then, I turn to the technical lead.

I ask them: *How long have we got before a rollback is required?*

See, there's a window of opportunity here to do some troubleshooting... before we need to rollback to the old firewalls to avoid further impacts to operations.

The technical lead says: *We've got 15 minutes.*

I call the IT Service Desk back and provide the update.

They inform me that clients are now calling in to say their apps are no longer accessible. They advise that we need to roll back.

I negotiate for five more minutes as the team scrambles to analyse what was happening. The Service Desk agrees.

But before long, the 15 minutes are up.

I tell the team we've got to wrap things up. That means we need to roll back and restore services... allowing traffic to flow through the old firewalls again. After all, the business could be losing as much as $50,000 every minute they're offline.

Again, the technical lead takes charge. They restore network services with the team as quickly as possible.

We know there will be consequences to a failed change. But we did the best we could... and we lived through another day.

Was it a massively stressful situation for me as a project manager? Well, any failed change is stressful and combined with impacts to operations, never leaves a good feeling.

There was only one thing that kept me grounded from the time the internet went down... up to the time we had restored services to stop the company from bleeding out $50K a minute.

And that was the quality of the team I had in the room with me. It was knowing that everybody in the team was 100% focused on what had to be done... and what their roles were. Because what happened here was something no one expected. We hadn't planned on making any mistakes... but at least I had assurance that every single member of the team was committed to understanding and solving the problem... or at least committed to executing our rollback plan.

See, we learn early on as part of our formal training that the Project Manager carries all accountability... from project kick off... through delivery... and all the way to closure. That means Project Managers are held accountable for everything related to the project (success or failure) as they control and manage everything and everyone... Yes, REALLY!

For this reason, many of us feel like we lead the life of a lone soldier. Alone in the trenches of the corporate world, delivering critical projects, and ultimately taking accountability of all things related to project delivery.

Just like with my story earlier. You know those three seconds I spent waiting for the Service Desk to inform me whether the network failure was causing any significant impacts? That moment of silence when that panic sets in, and everyone else is looking to me for answers or direction? Well, that part never gets any easier.

Because I know that I'm accountable for any impact the failed implementation of the firewalls may have had to our client's business. And I knew there was no way I could make excuses, or hide from it. All I could do was take responsibility... apologise... and commit to understanding what went wrong technically with the team and plan another implementation to get things across the line successfully next time.

But in reality... we are not actually lone soldiers. Or at least, we don't have to be. As long as we've got a team that is high-performing and committed... a team that trusts each other and we can rely on completely... then we feel confident in being able to deliver amazing outcomes for our clients.

I mean... you've seen Mission Impossible with Tom Cruise, right? I always think of delivering projects like "Mission Impossible"... which can only be made possible with incredible planning and teamwork. I always adopt that mindset when delivering projects now, just like that movie, and remind myself to imagine the unimaginable and expect the unexpected.

After all, projects are not always entirely predictable. Sometimes, they can be massively stressful, too.

And in those situations, I found that it's never healthy to struggle silently... and refuse to ask for help to solve your problems. That's why you have an entire team to back you up! See, many of us work so many hours with our teams getting projects across the line... that our team starts to become a temporary family... whom we can positively lean on for support.

And that's why you need to consider your team not just as a team... but as part of your support network.

Now, a good way to start creating a LIFE TEAM that could become your overall support network... is by looking at who you have in your network currently (within your proximity)... and review what value they bring to either your personal or professional life.

This can be a tough step... but also a necessary one... as it can help you determine how much effort, energy and time you should put towards them. Make sure you invest more time with the people that contribute most to your life and ensure that you are also there for them too.

I think about the people I have in my own support network currently and from a professional perspective... I have been able to form relationships with a broad range of incredible individuals and organisations. And I'm not just talking about my network in Project Management... but also in various fields of profession and interests, like Information Technology, Professional Speaking, Personal Development, Resilience, Mental Toughness, Health & Well-being, Martial Arts, Coaching, Business and Entrepreneurship.

From a personal perspective... I am also blessed to have formed some long lasting relationships with people who I know will always be there for me... as I will always be there for them too.

So now, let's move on to building YOUR support network.

The Psychographics of a Good Support Network

So, WHO do we want to add as part of our Support Network (Life Team)?

For starters, you need four key types of people in your network:

1. The Encourager

You've got to have someone in your corner to give you moral support when you need it. Someone who can cheer you on and sincerely believe in what you're doing.

Think of the German professional footballer, Manuel Neuer. Or any goalkeeper in a football team. They are the voices at the back telling everyone "Awesome work!" or "Go, go, go!" That's an Encourager.

Even though The Encourager may not contribute directly to your success... they will make sure that you stay focused on your mission. Take care of these people and don't take them for granted.

2. The Comforter

Robin Williams's character in Good Will Hunting is the perfect example of a Comforter. He's someone who can understand people and listen to them unload their problems at the end of a stressful day.

In Project Management, there are many times when you're going to have a bad day. And on those days, we all need people around us that are willing to just listen to us... allowing us to share our thoughts and get stuff off our minds... like the things that might be troubling us and the things we may be afraid of. The Comforter will be there for these moments... and they will listen to us without judgement.

And though they may not always be good at giving you advice... they will always make themselves available to listen, which is invaluable.

3. The Tactician

Now, these are the people who go beyond the comforter who just listens... as they will also help you create a plan and strategise on how to manage what's stressing you out. This could be someone that works in the same industry that you work... with the same experience, or it could be someone that you see as your mentor.

Think Wayne Bennett, an Australian professional rugby league coach who is widely regarded as one of the sport's greatest ever coaches and who's just unparalleled with his tactical brilliance.

Got any Wayne Bennetts in your life? Someone who can work out the perfect formula to beat what's keeping you up at night or challenging you?

If so, keep them close.

Tacticians ultimately have a level of experience that you can leverage. They have plenty of advice, and you can take whatever applies to your specific situation.

4. The Coach

One of the most valuable team members you can have as part of your Support Network... is a COACH. A coach is someone who has a vested interest in your success. Someone who forms a partnership with you based on commitment... which means this person will pull all the stops to help you achieve things that may be difficult to achieve by yourself.

Think Gregg Popovich, who has the most wins and is widely regarded as one of the greatest coaches in NBA history. He always knew how to encourage certain players... while knowing how to be tough on others. He always knew how to get the best performance out of the Spurs, no matter the year and who's playing.

That's the kind of person you definitely need on your team.

This person will support you at every level in building awareness... empowering you to always make the right choices and ultimately guides you as you go in the direction you want to go.

A term phrased by one of my mentors, Les Brown, which I have maintained at the forefront of my relationship-building is   **OQP** – Only Quality People!

Think about it...

So, as you go on and build a support network of your own... the most important tip I can give you from both my experience... and those of many others before me is this:

Surround yourself with people that lift you up and that see things in YOU that you don't see in yourself!

But that's not all.

Aside from looking at what kinds of people you should have on your support network, I also encourage you to look at people... who don't deserve to be there.

These are people you have in your life right now… who are keeping you where you are. Perhaps, they don't make you feel good or support what you want to do in life. Maybe they make you feel like you can't do what you've set out to do. And perhaps they push all their negative energy and own thoughts towards you… while they just coast through life, blissfully ignorant of the hustle you're in.

Keeping these people around just depletes your energy and attention… in favour of people who actually do think about your success and development.

Some of the kinds of people you should keep an eye out for that may be in your life… and really find a way to eliminate or avoid are:

The Whiners

Whiners make things hard by frequently complaining about the little things. Think Ross Geller from "Friends." Remember how he could instantly bring down an entire room with one of his patented and dejected "'Hi's"? And remember how he easily has the best, most comfortable, successful life among the six "Friends" and yet he's the one who's always complaining about things?

Well, that's just what whiners do. They always want more; they want their lives to be easier… and when it's not, they always think it's someone else's fault. These people drain the living energy out of us… their negativity is so contagious.

So, eliminate them from your team right away.

The Rocks

These people are totally fine with just… existing. They might as well be an actual rock. Sure, they won't try and drag you down, but they also won't try and lift you up. That's because they themselves have given up on dreaming… and have succumbed to the mindset of doing nothing in life… and just coasting along.

Think Jesse Pinkman in Breaking Bad before he got caught up in Heisenberg's meth-cooking ways. He had no dreams, no ambitions, no desire to work. He was perfectly fine just crashing on his friends' couches, without a care in the world as to what tomorrow might bring.

Just like the Whiner's negativity… the Rock's happy-go-lucky attitude is likewise contagious. If you spend enough time with them… you might find yourself wondering why you can't also just stay home all the time, relaxing and watching time pass you by. So, take the time to weed out Rocks from your support team.

The Cynics

No matter how great things are going, cynics will always have negative opinions about other people… and about the things other people do.

They almost solely exist to tell other people that their dreams and aspirations are not possible. Be aware that these are very toxic people that you do not need in your proximity or in your life!

Ever watched the show 'Curb Your Enthusiasm'? Seinfeld co-creator Larry David plays a magnificent cynic in the show. Entertaining to watch, for sure, but they're not fun to be around in real life. Cynics will do anything to bring you down with their daily doomsday mood… and it will just be a waste of energy trying to convince them that you're bound for great things.

So, just keep as far away from these people as possible!

The Blood Suckers

These types of people will suck the life out of you. They sit around sucking up valuable resources and are always looking for someone to suck the life out of.

I'm thinking of Rachel Green from 'Friends.' Sure, Ross was not a lot of fun with his whining and quite regressive views on society… but boy, did Rachel make his life *actually* hard! Rachel demanded so much from him (even during the time that they were supposedly ON A BREAK)… and employed a lot of push-pull tactics, keeping Ross hanging one day… and then breaking up his other relationships the next… just because she couldn't decide whether she still wanted to be with him or not!

In fact, after 10 seasons of dealing with Rachel, we could say Ross did have something real to whine about.

So, don't let blood suckers similar to Rachel Green into your life… let alone your Support Network.

69

Now, what if the whiners, rocks, cynics, and blood suckers in your life… are people you just can't weed out? Maybe they're family. Or some of your closest friends. Maybe even a neighbour who loves talking to you every morning.

Well, the only thing to do here is intentionally limit and minimise the time you spend with these people.

Another thing:

A lot of project management professionals believe that going to one Annual Conference per year suffices to be the extent of our relationship-building and creating our Support Network.

But as the founder of Project Managers Movement, a safe, non-judgemental professional community for Project Delivery Professionals, Corporate Leaders & Employees… I know for a fact that people have yet to experience and understand the TRUE Benefits of a REAL Support Network.

The multitude of people that I have been fortunate enough to have as part of the Project Managers Movement Community… come from all walks of life. From aspiring to seasoned project managers, right through to retirees in both project management & from the corporate world.

From them, I have observed that the power of a support network can be realised by just about anyone. Anyone who allows themselves to be genuinely and authentically interested in forming and building real relationships with others.

To me, a Support Network is synonymous to FAMILY.

And we both know the purpose of a FAMILY is to nurture and maintain the well-being of its members… and ideally offer structure, and safety as members mature and participate in the community.

So, now that you know what kinds of people you should have in your support network… and which ones to avoid at all costs… I don't want you to stop at just creating a support network. Instead, I want you to fully commit to having a great relationship with this newfound family of yours. Nurture your relationship with the best people in your network… and they'll surely reward you tenfold.

Value your Network

As you build your own support network, you will come to the realisation… that having a team to consider as family is a gift that must be treasured. The network you will create will be made up of different types of people… coming together to support each other… leverage from each other's experiences… and exchange opportunities for both personal and professional growth or development.

Then, you will truly start to see the power of what can be possible… when you consciously start focusing on building relationships at the core of your existence day to day.

Having a strong support network is something I was fortunate to realise early on. And upon realising just how powerful a project manager can be with a reliable support system… I committed myself to helping other professionals in the industry build their own networks too.

So, let me share with you my vision for Project Managers Movement:

"To be the Professional Community of choice both Nationally and Globally for Project Management Professionals, Corporate Leaders and Employees, where individuals can be themselves, connect with others, inspire through achievement, live with integrity, show courage in the face of adversity while on a journey of continual self-development in the pursuit of Self-Mastery."

And I will leave with you a quote from Jim Rohn:

"Your network is your Net Worth."

I completely agree. The people you surround yourself with can completely change your life one way or the other. So, choose wisely… and value your network once you have it built.

What I Learned From Running an IT Consulting Business: HEALTH

As my business gained momentum and matured... things got extremely busy.

As is the case for Project Management Professionals in the throes of Project Execution Phase. We were spending most of our time coordinating the team/s... ensuring quality work... keeping track of resources... and updating customers & stakeholders.

I did test some theories about working hard during this time too, of course. What else would a learner do?

I thought:

If I worked 24/7, could I make more money?

The answer was YES, BUT...

Over time it would not be sustainable... and will ultimately take its toll on my mental and physical being...

And that's exactly what happened.

I discovered that because of my business, I was starting to forget about ME.

Overall, I found that I was dropping some key elements to what I believe constitutes Happiness and Harmony in one's world, which for me was: HEALTH, BALANCE, GROWTH, AND BUSINESS.

As things in my professional life started to snowball... and as business started doing really well, I found myself in the background... taking care of everyone else but at the same time having to sacrifice some of the good things that were critical to my wellbeing.

I was getting up earlier and going to bed later. I missed dinners with the family. I had virtually no time for rest and recreation.

This *busyness*... which turned into exhaustion from always running on adrenaline... started to have a negative impact on my personal life and relationships.

Not only did I end up neglecting my family - my relationships with friends were also becoming extremely difficult to maintain.

Eventually, people would stop inviting me out, as they knew I was busy running the business. Perhaps they also grew too tired of my constant refusals to hang out. Even stopping to smell the roses for a minute became a struggle for me to do... as the unhealthy habits I had formed became very embedded into my daily routine.

My personal development... which used to keep me invigorated and focused, now all of a sudden had stopped completely.

All the things that used to inspire and drive my growth (like picking up new learnings, gaining new certifications, etc.) had also been put on the back burner.

To be perfectly honest, I never would have thought this would happen to me. Needless to say, realising what was happening rattled me significantly.

And that's not all. It's not just my personal development that suffered through all the busyness. Although thriving with work, the business struggled in many aspects. As you know, client fulfilment is just one part of a business's daily operations. As virtually all my efforts were focused on that... I started to neglect other aspects of the business... like maintaining good relationships among my team members. Ultimately, working too much caused me to self-destruct and kept my work at suboptimal levels.

TIPS:

1. Without your HEALTH at the core of your daily focus, you will never excel in what you do for an extended period of time. Though you might not feel like you're already having health issues… the real impact of what you're doing to your body will make itself felt years into the future… and even more so as you move into so-called retirement.

As described in the book "The Slight Edge" by Jeff Olson, it's the little things we do EACH day, be they good or bad… which will determine the long-term outcome or result of what we're doing. For many of us, we make daily choices about our health that will not have a significant effect in our lives for the next 40 years. Until we hit the 41st year and all of a sudden, we're afflicted with conditions… which we could blame no one else for but ourselves.

2. If you are seeking real Happiness and Harmony in your life, here's what you have to do:

First, you must take control of your world and BALANCE your focus… to include things that build on your experiences, like spending quality time with friends and family. Then, combine those experiences with growth opportunities… to do things which could maintain your health… continual learning… and physical/spiritual/mental fitness. Finally, add an element of Contribution. This means giving back into the world around you through your career and to your family or broader community.

3. Making Personal Development part of who you are is another critical element to not only GROWTH… but also to a rewarding and balanced life. It is also the conduit to seeing inside your soul… and embracing your uniqueness… and LOVING YOURSELF unconditionally!

4. Lastly, BUSINESS can be a rewarding experience. But as with all things, it is not for everyone.

Sure, the skills needed to run a successful business are not special or unattainable. But it does require you to be comfortable in building a team that supports YOU… along with having a mindset of continuous improvement and being comfortable with change, risk, and pressure.

So many of us, including myself, find ourselves becoming "Lone Soldiers". We run projects and we make ourselves feel like we need to carry the burden of solving problems on our own. But when you open your mind and heart… you can learn to leverage the help of those around you. This will then create incredible results… that wouldn't have been possible if you were truly all on your own.

CHAPTER 6

Seek Self-Mastery

Say what you want about the Red Queen in Alice in Wonderland… but she did make some excellent points about the nature of life.

Remember when she told Alice: *"Here, you see, it takes all the running you can do to keep in the same place."?*

That hit hard.

The Red Queen Effect is something I've observed with my own two eyes. As we get older, we have more responsibilities. People expect more from us. And as we deliver more and more value out into the world, the more it seems to demand from us.

So, one day, you're working harder than ever before, thinking to yourself:

"Oh, it's going to get easier soon."

Yet, it never does.

In fact, things just keep getting harder. Until you realise that you're running faster and faster… just to stay in the same place. You're working harder… yet your life is not really improving in proportion to the energy and effort you're putting into things.

I was on that relentless marathon for a long time… trying to catch up. To what, I couldn't tell you.

But I bet I'm not the only one experiencing this Red Queen Effect on a daily basis.

From the time we are born, right through to early adulthood… we get exposed to so many things we need to comply with.

Cultural norms. Community expectations. Social functions. Family rules. Religious guidance. Beliefs that were passed on to us from previous generations. It seems we are always running to meet all of these external qualifications to somehow be acceptable as people.

We don't even question whether it's right or wrong. We just get caught up in this whirlwind of expectations and demands... and we just go with the flow.

And then, we reach full-fledged adulthood. Suddenly, we've got bills to pay.

The metrics change, but all the same - we are constantly being assessed for the things we do, the things we don't do... and the things we have or don't have. So much so that we're always having to do more... just to survive and stay in the same place.

We get our first car... and immediately feel the pressure to buy a nicer one. We start a cushy job, and we immediately feel like we should work hard for a promotion. We get our own place... and immediately feel the need to buy a $3,000 knife set to elevate the kitchen space.

After all, that's what everybody else is doing. And for the longest time, I thought that if I just did what everyone else around me was doing... then I would be alright.

Until you actually get all those things... reach the pinnacle of success... and that's when you feel empty.

That's when you realise that happiness is not about the car. Or the promotion. Or the most expensive cutlery set you can find. Instead, it's about who you're singing in the car with on those long drives home. It's about who you're popping champagne bottles with once you do get that promotion. It's about who you're eating dinner with, $3,000 cutlery set or not.

That's when you realise all this running around meeting everyone's expectations and demands did not serve you well. And finally, against all odds, you start to ignore the noise of the outside world... and start to focus on within.

What does YOUR heart tell you to do?

What kind of life do YOU really want to have?

What should YOU be doing to achieve that kind of life?

As you ask and answer these questions… you take your first steps away from what the rest of the world demands you to be… and you take your first steps towards self-mastery.

The Massive Market for Self-Mastery

There's a popular Italian proverb that goes like this:

Every morning, the lion wakes up in the jungle, thinking to himself:

Today's a new day. I'm going to have to run fast. Gotta be at least faster than the slowest gazelle. Or else, I won't be able to eat, and I'll die.

Elsewhere in the jungle, the gazelle wakes up at the same time, thinking:

Today's a new day. I'm going to have to run fast. Gotta be faster than the lion… or else, they'd catch me… and I'd die!

So, it doesn't matter if you think you're a lion… or a gazelle. When you wake up, start running!

This is exactly how most of us live our lives.

We wake up… and we start running.

We're either like the lion, who's chasing something. Or like the gazelle, who's simply running for survival.

Here's the thing, though…

All of us would like to think we're the lion - fierce, strong, and always chasing after something it truly wants - a live gazelle to feast on.

But in reality… can you honestly tell me that you're chasing after something you *truly* want?

78

Are you chasing a gazelle because you really want to… or because it's what society has told you to want? Could it be possible that you're chasing after a gazelle… when what you really want is deer? Or even elk?

Point is… fulfilment always starts with choosing the right thing to chase. Think long and hard if the things you're working hard to achieve right now… are things that you actually want. Because if you're chasing things that you've only been told by society to want… then there can never be fulfilment from achieving all that.

On the flip side of the coin, we're not always running in pursuit of something. That means we're not always the lion - sometimes, we're the gazelle in the story. We're running away from something bad that might happen if we don't.

We're running so the bank won't foreclose on our mortgage. Or so that someone we care about won't think less of us. Or so we could impress the people who have always looked down on us.

Now, some of those fears are real (just like the gazelle's fear of the lion in the story) but a lot of them are mere fabrications of society, as well. We fear judgement, for instance, because the world around us can be a harsh critic. Thus, we are engineered to do things the same way everyone else does them – so we don't stand out and invite judgement.

So, apart from chasing things that are right for you… make sure you're only running away from things that genuinely scare you. Don't keep running blindly forward… just because someone says there's a lion behind you. You've got to see that lion for yourself, so you can decide for yourself whether there's a real reason for you to run away.

Otherwise, you'd forever be stuck under the Red Queen Effect - where you're running faster and faster and faster - just to stay in the same place.

What I need you to do is take stock of your life.

How fast are you running at the moment?

And what are you chasing? Are these things that truly bring you happiness and fulfilment?

And what are you running away from? Are these things that genuinely scare you… or are they just fears you have… because they were imposed upon you?

I believe it was Mark Twain who said:

"I've suffered a great many catastrophes in my life. Most of them never happened."

And this is true for many of us. Most of the suffering that will happen to us in this life… will be imagined. Which is exactly why the art of self-mastery matters. Because if you could master your own thoughts… your own needs… your own fears… then you will never suffer from imagined misfortune.

Interestingly, more and more people are coming to the same realisations… surrounding personal development and self-mastery.

A report published by Grand View Research found that the market size for global personal development was valued at a whopping USD $38.2 billion in 2019.

And as if that's not impressive enough, that value is expected to grow further at an annual rate of 5.1%... from 2020 to 2027.

Needless to say, there is definitely a trend of increased consciousness around self-improvement… and the pursuit of genuine fulfilment and happiness. The number of people still willing to run for nothing is depleting by the day. Instead, we are all looking for ways to improve on physical, mental, emotional, and spiritual fitness.

Heightened self-awareness is also taking a front seat now… with things like emotional intelligence, our daily habits, rituals, values, and beliefs… being acknowledged for shaping our day-to-day behaviours.

I vividly remember back in 2008, I was still running my IT Support & Consulting business.

You know the drill.

3:30 a.m.

I wake up, check my diary for appointments, and complete some initial planning for the day ahead.

Then, I jump into my car and head towards the Northern Beaches for my first client visit of the day.

Now, here's the part I haven't told you yet:

As it was an hour and a half drive to this client's site… I had plenty of time to think… and my brain frequently went into overdrive. I wouldn't just think about what I was supposed to be doing that day - oh no. I'd be thinking about the week ahead… all the different things that the team were working on… and random ideas on how to improve and refine our way of working.

TIME was my most precious commodity (still is). I would live by the clock and die by the clock as my team had to keep appointments across Greater Sydney.

My clients loved the way I worked!

A friendly attitude… always full of energy… and always committed to genuinely satisfying the customer and getting the job done for them… while making lots of friends and acquaintances along the way.

So why was I struggling?

Business was thriving. My clients loved me. Everything I need is provided for.

So why wasn't I happy?

After making an audit of my life, I realised… I was being challenged both physically and mentally!

So much so... that I wasn't enjoying my work anymore.

I was always tired and had no time for myself personally.

With the never-ending workload mounting (a good problem to have in business)... I was looking for other things to blame.

What was going to be my scapegoat?

Was it my customers being too demanding?

My employees not working hard enough?

Or the fact that customers didn't always pay on time... preventing me from re-investing in the business to get more help?

I know I battled with this for some time, questioning all the things around me... and always looking for reasons why I found myself in those situations I ended up in.

This one day, my ever observant wife made me aware that I was starting to break some of my own rules... as a result of the things that were playing out in my business.

I was paying my staff before I was paying myself. I was paying my suppliers before I was chasing my debtors. I was giving up my personal time to catch up on business paperwork. And I was also giving up my personal development and training regime... because I just didn't have time to do it all anymore.

Throughout this entire process, I never once thought that the problem was ME.

I always just considered myself a victim to the circumstances. I pictured myself caught in a wild water rapids ride... taking me downstream but also wearing me down.

Every time I look at my CV and look at my key qualifications, I always see that GAP between 2001 and 2012 where everything just stopped for me... at least from a training and development perspective.

It's a reminder of one of my lowest moments as a LEARNER.

Thankfully, I became more conscious of what was happening to me.

I started to identify some things I was chasing that I didn't really want to chase. And things I was running away from even though they don't really scare me. Armed with this knowledge, I was able to streamline my life.

I spent more of my energy on things I enjoyed doing.

More of my time on people that I truly care about.

And more of my resources on chasing things that go into my personal development.

That's how I was able to become a master of myself.

And you can do it, too.

Maslow's Hierarchy of Needs

Ever been in a purple patch?

You know... that period of time when you're very lucky, very successful, and nothing seems to go wrong?

I've been in a few of those myself.

And if there's one thing I can tell you about purple patches... it's that they don't last forever.

It's not really the case that luck runs out... or our successes are merely balanced by our fair share of failures.

What I mean is... purple patches don't go on and on... because we as humans are evolutionary beings. We tend to adapt to our environment. So, when things have been pretty awesome for a while... we tend to settle in. What used to be awesome now just feels normal.

Eventually, you no longer feel like you're on a purple patch. You've grown accustomed to it... so you start to want more - or at least something else. So, you play yourself into the right position once more... until you hit that patch that makes things awesome again for a little while.

And then, the cycle repeats.

Now, why is it that we as humans go through these micro-evolutions of wanting, achieving, and then wanting more?

Well, Maslow has explained it all in his Simplified Hierarchy of Needs.

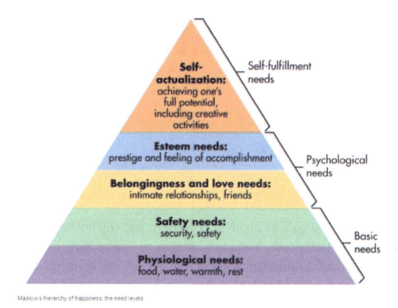

Maslow's hierarchy of happiness: the need levels

According to Maslow, all humans have evolving needs.

Looking at the model above, we've all got basic needs, psychological needs, and self-fulfilment needs.

Here's how we micro-evolve through these needs.

First, we aim for survival.

As a result, we achieve our basic needs... and we feel pretty awesome for a while.

But then, when the ability to enjoy all your basic needs becomes a normal occurrence in your life... you start to feel like something else is missing.

That's when you start working to meet your psychological needs. When you achieve it, you once again feel pretty awesome for a while. But then, having psychological fulfilment becomes an ordinary component of your life... so you again feel like something else is missing.

Finally, you strive to have your self-fulfilment needs met.

Now, let's take a look at what each of these needs actually look like in real life.

1. Physiological Needs

Food. Water. Warmth. Rest.

Ah, the most basic of needs.

And yet, how many of us can say without batting an eye that we have all our physiological needs met?

Believe me. You could be highly successful... and still not be able to enjoy your physiological needs. You already know my story. Busy as I was with my IT Support & Consulting business, I frequently missed meals. I crawled to bed late and woke up at 3:30 in the morning like clockwork!

See, just because you technically have access to your physiological needs... doesn't mean they're actually being met!

So, answer me this:

How consistent are your eating habits? What about the quality of food that you're consuming? Are you drinking enough water? And, the most crucial of them all - how many nights do you spend lying awake, worried about the next day... compromising your sleep and thus compromising your immune system?

Maslow considers physiological needs as the most essential of our needs. If you're not meeting any of these... you've got to think of ways to address the deficits.

2. Safety Needs

After your physiological needs come your safety needs.

From a very young age, most of us were afforded safe and predictable environments to grow and learn. That's why we typically react with fear or anxiety... whenever we have to be in a place or a situation that doesn't feel safe nor predictable.

Like when I had customers with outstanding accounts preventing me from paying myself... that created that sense of fear and anxiety around my own security.

So, is there anything in your life that makes you feel unsafe at the moment?

How about your sense of security? Do you live paycheck to paycheck?

How much of a safety net do you have right now? And how much do you actually need?

And what would you do if (heaven forbid) something big happens... and it affects your ability to earn and provide for your family?

Safety needs are still considered part of our basic needs... so you've got to find a way to meet them. Otherwise, you will find it harder to achieve the remaining things that sit on top of this pyramid.

3. Love and Belonging Needs

Maslow says the next need in the hierarchy is love and belongingness.

This can be achieved through intimate relationships with your partner... family... or friends.

If you remember, working extremely long hours meant I was neglecting the relationships I had with friends, family and also many times with my wife. And I can't tell you honestly what would have happened to me if I hadn't turned things around... and ended up losing these very important people in my life. My world would have shattered.

So, if you're in the same situation where you've been neglecting your personal relationships... please, please please... do something about it soon.

4. Esteem Needs

Our esteem needs involve the need to feel good about oneself.

And it consists of two elements. The first is a feeling of self-confidence - hence, it comes from within. The second involves feeling valued by others.

That's right.

Knowing that our achievements and contributions are appreciated and recognised by others is likewise important.

At the height of my business, my clients only had nice things to say about me. Yet, I couldn't stop questioning my self-confidence. Call it inferiority complex or imposter syndrome... but a part of me did not feel accomplished... despite the external validation I frequently got.

If you're the same way, you've got your work cut out for you. Keep reading, because the next part of this chapter will be all about taking back control of your life through self-mastery.

But before we go there, let's cap off Maslow's Hierarchy of Needs with the last, topmost need in the pyramid:

5. Self-Actualisation Needs

Self-actualisation relates to feeling like we are living life to its full potential.

Now, self-actualisation looks different for each of us.

For me, as of writing, self-actualisation means that I am consciously feeling, living, and believing that I am doing what I am meant to be doing in my life.

It may be a work in progress... but I am in control!

Achieving full self-actualisation is relatively rare.

But some of the people we know who managed to get there would be Abraham Lincoln, Albert Einstein, and Mother Teresa.

It's going to be a long journey to the top of this hierarchy. Yes, you can have it all... but you've got to be patient. You've got to be patient... and you've actually gotta do the work.

Because no one else in your life will be responsible for making sure that all your needs are met daily.

Only you.

But a great first step is to decide what your self-actualised self looks like.

When all is said and done, what kind of person do you want to be? How would you like to be remembered? How do you know if you are fully, 100% self-fulfilled?

Once you have that vision of what you ultimately want to be... then it's time to take the next step: taking back control and full accountability of your own life... in order to become a master of your SELF and eventually become the person you've always wanted to be.

Take Back Control with Self-Mastery

I took many, many, many steps on the road to self-mastery.

But every single one of those steps was well worth it.

Because as of today, I am no longer the same person who used to let his life run on autopilot. I live my days intentionally... eating when I'm supposed to... coming home to dinner with my wife on time... and constantly allowing myself to develop, both personally and professionally.

It has been an incredible journey... and I can't wait to see you go through it yourself!

So, to give you a proper head start to that long and winding journey to mastering the SELF and becoming the person you were always meant to become...

Let me share with you the steps I took to take back control and be accountable for my own life:

These steps are divided into two phases:

- Self-Awareness and Discovery; and
- Self-Development/Personal Development

Let's start with Phase 1 - **Self-Awareness and Discovery.**

To truly master the SELF, you've got to know the SELF.

You've got to discover where you are right now. How your health is doing. How your thoughts and emotions are impacting your behaviours. And what your strengths and weaknesses are.

Here are some actionable steps I took... which you might find helpful in your own self-discovery:

#1: Slow down

Understanding who you are requires careful, deliberate thought. Which is why you can't be like I was, with the highway hypnosis... and the losing control of what was happening in my life... and the relentless rushing from one place to another.

You've got to slow down. Take time each day for yourself to switch off and clear your mind.

Some of the things I do are daily mindfulness practices... walks in the park... or even just stopping and sitting in the sun to read a good book.

These moments of silence and space are what you need to become more aware of what's happening within.

#2. Listen to your body

Our bodies are an incredible creation. We've got five senses that help us understand and perceive the world around us. And yet, we don't always see things that are right in front of us… nor hear what our friends, family, or associates are directly trying to tell us.

I've been there. I had ears but didn't hear my wife's reminders for the longest time. I had eyes, but I failed to see that I was already sacrificing way too much for my business's success.

But once I leveraged my senses to discover more about myself in relation to the world around me… that's when I discovered fulfilment in living a more balanced life.

#3. Leverage your strengths, weaknesses, and personality

For the longest time, I had no idea what my strengths and weaknesses were… apart from what my friends, family, teachers, or work colleagues told me.

But understanding what makes up YOU as a person can truly make a profound difference in your life. Because the moment I learned what my strengths and weaknesses were, I also started to live life with more intention - doing more of the things I'm good at… and delegating tasks that I'm not so good at. No time wasted, and very minimal stress.

There are many different assessments you could take to find out more about who you are. To get you started on this specific part of your self-discovery… check out the Clifton Strengths Assessment… which will help you identify your top strengths.

#4. Decide to become more conscientious

As you discover more of who you truly are… and as you rediscover what you believe in… how you speak… how you think… how you behave in different situations… you're bound to have an awakening.

This is where you start to SEE so much of your life that you didn't realise previously. Just like I discovered how much of my behaviour during stressful situations were shaped by my childhood... when I had to deal with so many Brules! (Remember Brules?). Knowing that, I was able to become more conscientious.

I started consciously refusing to let my upbringing dictate how I behave today... and I can tell you it feels like unlocking a superpower. This ability to inject conscious thought into every decision... every reaction... and every action you make... is really something else. Once you're able to do that, you know you're ready to take the next steps towards Self-Mastery.

That means you can now move on to Phase 2: **Self Development and Personal Development.**

See, my concern about the self-awareness and discovery phase... is that it doesn't require us to take any real ACTION.

It's all about learning and collecting insight about certain things in our life. But I know you know that without action... all those insights and learnings you gained about yourself... will not lead to any significant change in your life.

I know this, because it was only when I used my self-awareness to take better action in my life... that I really started to satisfy my self-fulfilment needs.

Now, you also know that the Self Development & Personal Development phase wasn't always so easy for me. I struggled for a really long time with making time for myself... what with all the commitments I had!

But something shifted inside of me when I realised I had gotten so good at fulfilling other people's needs... but never my own!

So, I decided to do better and acted on the following steps:

#1. Understanding the LOCUS OF CONTROL

Locus of Control refers to our perception of what underlying causes affect the events in our life.

Do you believe that your destiny is controlled by forces you have no control over? May it be God, the universe, or any other powerful being? That means you have an external locus of control. Which is what I had for the longest time - the reason why I wasn't doing anything related to self-development. I had all the external reasons to blame, anyway.

But if you believe that your destiny is but the aggregate result of all your actions and decisions... then it means you have an internal locus of control. And that's good!

Generally, it's a lot healthier to perceive that you have control over your own destiny... because that means changing it is well within your power.

#2. Set boundaries

As Project Delivery Professionals, Corporate Leaders & Employees... it is important to set boundaries in your professional life.

Someone with healthy boundaries understands that having clear expectations helps in two ways:

- It establishes what behaviour you will accept from other people, and
- It establishes what behaviour other people can expect from you.

Many of us could work 24/7 at the expense of other aspects of our lives... and still not get all the work we need done.

That's why it's important to set boundaries around how much time you spend on your JOB... and make time for your relationships and your personal development.

#3. Take baby steps

Reality dictates that we must acknowledge all areas of our lives in order to lead a balanced and fulfilling existence.

As you start to focus more on yourself, remember to progressively make the changes needed to support your Personal Development, too… as it's the little things we do consistently over time that make a significant impact in our lives.

I know for me, I started with dedicating one hour every week on a specific day to work on myself.

But the interesting thing was that… as I committed to myself, to taking the action within that one hour per week… my mindset began to change. My vision of myself also changed, and I started to think that anything was possible. You just gotta start with baby steps.

#4: Make Yourself your OWN Highest Priority

When you start to shift your focus on the most important things in YOUR life, the magic starts to happen.

You find that you will automatically stop making excuses… and start to look forward to doing the work that makes you better.

In effect, your vision of yourself also starts to shift.

All of a sudden, you see things which were not visible to you previously and you start to do things which you thought you would never have done.

Additionally… Personal Development attracted many different people into my life. Some of them even became the catalyst for the change I created in my life. And they also supported me in having the courage to take the first steps into the unknown… which helped turn my possibilities into a reality.

Self-mastery through self-development and personal development. This is how I kept myself evolving with this ever-changing world. To this day, I revisit these steps to further understand myself… and see if there's anything

I can improve on… to ultimately achieve success, happiness, and fulfilment in my own life.

Les Brown, who you already know to be one of my life mentors, said this about Self-Mastery:

"Work on yourself continually, never be satisfied!"

As you continue to work on yourself, you will begin to expand your vision of yourself.

You will begin to work towards Self-Mastery, and you will begin to see it reflect itself in all the dimensions of your life.

Your mental life, your physical life, your social life, in your relationships, and your monetary life.

Change your habits, change your LIFE!

What I Learned From Running an IT Consulting Business: SURVIVAL & RESILIENCE

As you run your projects, you'd find that pain can be a very effective teacher.

For many Project Delivery Professionals and Corporate Leaders, we find ourselves slaves to the pain of running challenging projects. That's why we have to learn how to use the pain… instead of letting it use us.

In my own consulting business, I came so close to BURNOUT that it became obvious the PAIN was using ME!

It was during this time that I learnt my biggest lesson about: SURVIVAL, STRESS & RESILIENCE

As many parts of my business spiralled out of control and were getting mismanaged through lack of knowledge, lack of consciousness, and negative behaviour on my part, I kept going.

It became a game of survival that I thought I was playing really well.

Until I was hit with this wonderful thing called STRESS.

(And I'm not being sarcastic when I say it's wonderful!)

See, stress can be either positive (eustress) or negative (distress). But the body itself cannot physically distinguish between distress or eustress. The distinction is dependent on your experience… as the individual experiencing the stress.

I can definitely vouch for that, I was completely oblivious to what I was experiencing and, in my view, negative or positive, it was just how it was.

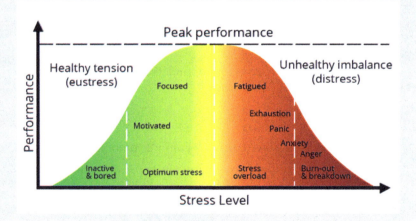

Distress, or negative stress, has a negative impact… and is usually overwhelming and out of a person's control. On the other hand, eustress has a positive correlation with life satisfaction and hope because it fosters challenge and motivation towards a goal.

For project managers, every single event can cause either distress or eustress, depending on how we as individuals interpret the information received by our brains.

And although I was familiar with some of the methods which could be used to reduce stress and increase my tolerance to it… I was doing too many other things wrong.

I remember that day when I could not get out of bed due to extreme burnout. It was a strange feeling and I still remember it like it was yesterday. My wife looking over at me in bed wondering what was going on, as I sobbed, confused, and in a state of complete mental exhaustion.

In a way, I am thankful for that moment of sheer stress… as this became the point in time which transformed my business and life.

I have since become a PR6 Driven Certified Resilience Coach. That means I now have access to all the tools that can help me thrive.

But more importantly, I leverage this certification to help my teams, coaching students and Project Delivery peers become aware of not only how to manage stress… but to work daily on building RESILIENCE as a long-term method of managing negative stress… which they may experience in their lifetime.

TIPS:

1. Although going into SURVIVAL mode is almost an automatic and natural response to stress… pressure…or perceived danger… you've got to be careful with it. When you're constantly in survival mode, there's a very high chance that you will adopt behaviours that do not serve you in a positive way.

So, always acknowledge and document your daily rituals and/or responses to situations so you have an opportunity to make changes... if and when required.

2. Stress management is a critical element to managing your stress while running Projects.

Relieve stress through physical relaxation techniques like exercising, walking, running etc. Psychological methods can also be utilised to reduce stress. Try meditation, mindfulness, and positive thinking... as ways to reduce your response to stress.

For me, simply taking some time out in nature regularly works wonders. Physically moving away from a stressful situation and filling my lungs with some fresh air through 6-8 deep breaths... also resets me and allows me to come back to the situation more objectively.

3. RESILIENCE is the ability to positively respond to adversity.

Admittedly, I didn't always realise that resilience is an important part of addressing the challenges we face every day... including those from relationships, work, traffic, etc.

Having low resilience can result in small challenges feeling like disasters, while big challenges can really knock you down for a long time.

But having high resilience will help you grow through adversity, so that you constantly become stronger through learning and change... while also helping you focus on your sense of purpose and meaning. In the end, this allows you to achieve your goals, regardless of what adversity you may face.

All these things can then help you thrive... as you deliver more complex and challenging projects with your teams.

CHAPTER 7

Propel Your Career as a Project Management Professional

Let me share with you an experience that still gives me traumatic flashbacks to this day.

Many years ago, I was in a meeting room with my project team. Picture me sitting there looking frustrated and stressed. Imagine that the only thing missing was a camera to comically zoom into my bewildered face and a voice over that says:

"Yep, that's me. You're probably wondering how I ended up here."

Because honestly, I was wondering the same thing.

See, the main agenda for our meeting that day was for the project architects to turn over the project design — also known as the blueprint — to my team... so that we can start implementing the project in two weeks' time.

Two weeks would have been just enough for my team to study the design and make our preparations for project delivery.

But then...

The lead solution architect comes to the meeting to tell me that the design is not yet ready.

It was the deadline and they're not ready. No warnings, no issues, no escalations... nothing!

Sure, a few days before the meeting, someone told me there was a design element that needed to be modified... but I was under the impression it was all minor and manageable. But on the due date, I got told the architects needed a few days to finish a redesign.

Immediately, I started thinking about the spin-off effects of this delay in the design milestone of the project. Without the final blueprint, my team wouldn't be able to deliver the actual, physical implementation of the technology we were supposed to launch for the client in two weeks' time.

And we had things hedging on getting that implementation done!

We had already raised an IT change request in the client's system, but since we won't be able to implement the new system within the pre-agreed timeline... we were facing extra costs in the delivery of the project.

And so I was torn between two equally dreadful options.

Either I give the architects the time they need for the redesign — like I had a choice here — which meant I had to work extra hours to reschedule and replan the entire project delivery to try and keep it on track...

Or, understand technically what the implications of delivering to the initial design would be without waiting for the required redesign... but it was also much riskier taking this option. After all, even miniscule changes to the design can have massive ramifications to its implementation.

While I weighed those two options as a fledging, up and coming project manager, I learned a hard lesson that day about the immense importance of the Project Manager's role... in delivering successful projects for clients and businesses.

I realised just how big a responsibility Project Managers had in playing a lead role in planning, executing, monitoring, controlling, and closing out projects. It dawned on me that day that Project Managers are accountable to deliver the entire project to scope... manage their teams and resources... and not to mention also manage the project budget.

In other words, the success or failure of a project literally falls squarely on the Project Manager's shoulders.

And so whenever I had the chance to rub shoulders with Project Managers who were running multimillion-dollar projects but still came across as very grounded and humble people... I get taken back to that day in the meeting room... facing what seemed a simple decision as a young Project Manager.

I started to observe how those successful Project Managers were leading... especially noticing them leading from behind and creating the conditions that allowed their teams to shine, take charge of decision-making, but always ready to step in when required. Knowing very well how many of those mind-splitting decisions they must have had to make to get to where they are... I started seeing Project Managers as unsung heroes in their own right.

And so I set the benchmark for what kind of Project Manager I aspired to be.

I challenged myself not only to progress my career, but to propel it beyond just being an average Project Manager.

I aspired to be better at every aspect of Project Management... and become the best Project Management Professional I could be.

The first step I took on that journey... was to break down the roles and responsibilities of Project Managers, and I came up with a pretty long list — a long list of things I strived hard to get better at.

The Responsibilities of a Project Manager

Let me share with you the list I came up with when I thought about the roles and responsibilities of Project Managers. This is the same list you'd want to keep on hand... as you start to propel your career as a Project Management Professional.

So, a Project Manager is in charge of:

- Scope Management
- Overall Planning and Scheduling
- Resource Management & Planning
- Estimating Time and Cost
- Developing and managing budget and delivery timelines
- Managing Risks and Issues
- Controlling, Monitoring and Reporting
- Team Management, Motivation & Leadership

These all seem pretty standard, don't you think?

Yeah, I thought so, too.

These are skills you'd easily pick up while training to become a Project Manager. In fact, if you're already considering a career in Project Management... I'm sure you already have some of these skills in your arsenal.

So, the question really is:

How do you effectively apply what you know about these areas of project management… in a way that allows you to master projects effectively? How do you distinguish your skills from that of an average Project Management Professional… just like the unsung heroes I mentioned earlier?

Well, here's what I can tell you:

When I asked myself the same two questions… I came up with two critical areas that project managers need to dial up… to be able to do extraordinary work: **health** and **mindset.**

The Two Critical Areas for Project Managers

A few days before writing this, I've been tormented by migraines so severe, it made looking at my screen virtually impossible. My temple throbbed as if a screwdriver was forcing its way into my head. Back in the day, I would have "powered through" the pain and continued working as if nothing is bothering me.

But instead of making the problem worse by doing what I would normally do… I have been shutting off my computer and lying down when I need to.

Why?

It's because I have decided to take care of myself and allow my body to heal and recover when it gives me the signs that it needs to.

See, in 2021, I had my first experience with kidney stones.

And I can definitely confirm that when your health lets you down, you will struggle with everything else. I know from experience that as individuals, we often strive for success by adopting habits that are often detrimental to our health. And some of us only understand the value of health when we start to lose it.

I know I used to take my health and body for granted… and I was lucky I was able to stop doing it before it was too late. Some aren't so lucky. They overexert themselves until they're broken or in pain. Then, they try to undo years of unhealthy habits, often to no avail.

So, as someone who escaped that tragic fate by the skin of my teeth… let me share with you some basic tips on how to take better care of your health.

I hope you take these tips to heart, because without good health... you won't be able to carry out the multitude of responsibilities of a good project manager.

Here are some of my basic **health tips:**

1. Always keep in mind that without our health, we are nothing.
2. Respect and take care of your body as if it were a temple.
3. Go in for at least a yearly check-up... and go see your doctor the moment something comes up. Make it a habit to listen to your body and what it needs.
4. Movement is critical to your health, so make regular exercise a part of your daily routine.
5. Eat fresh, healthy foods and drink plenty of water.

Now, we can't have a discussion about health without mentioning mental health, too.

See, having a great mindset and a solid state of mind is fundamental to propelling your career as a Project Management Professional.

After all, years of delivering many different types of technology-based projects for customers in various industries taught me one thing that's common with all these projects:

Not everything will go according to plan. Whether big or small, something almost always goes wrong. Just think back to the story I told you earlier about the project design getting delayed. I carefully planned and planned every single detail of that project... but some things are just out of our control. And when those things don't go as planned... it will take a mental toll on you.

For starters, your clients and the rest of the market will cast judgement on you for whatever goes wrong... even if it's not entirely your fault. You're in charge, after all.

And it is at this point that MINDSET becomes crucial. Because while you can't control how other people will judge you... you are in full control of how you respond to it. Do you take the criticism in your stride and use it as fuel to do better... or do you take it personally to the point of doing things you're not responsible for... just so you won't look incompetent?

Well, the answer ultimately depends on what kind of mindset you have.

Carol Susan Dweck, an American author and psychologist, discovered that there are two different mindsets that a person can have. You either have a 'fixed' mindset... or a 'growth' mindset. And the kind of mindset you have ultimately dictates how you approach life and work.

On one hand, Dweck observed that people with a fixed mindset believe that their intelligence and abilities are fixed — and therefore limited. That means they tend to give up quickly when things are not working well. Because when something doesn't work the first time, they immediately assume that they just don't have the ability to make it happen. In other words, people with fixed mindsets tend not to have very accurate views of their own performance and abilities. As such, they tend to evaluate situations solely in terms of whether or not it made them appear intelligent... or acceptable to others. Worse, their tendency to attribute failure to their own lack of ability causes them to lose confidence and feel overwhelmed easily. In effect, they have a tendency to be more risk-averse and self-conscious to a fault.

On the other hand, Dweck observed that people with a growth mindset believe they have the ability to succeed in whatever they do... through their own sheer effort. As such, they are eager to learn. And if something doesn't work the first time around, they will simply try harder and persevere until they *make it work.*

See, people with a growth mindset tend to have a more accurate view of their abilities, which makes them more open to feedback — even if it's unflattering. They very rarely react to things on an emotional level... and are thus more capable of carrying out a more logical analysis of any situation. This helps them avoid the thinking errors we are prone to make... when we respond to things emotionally.

Even the prospect of failing does not faze people with a growth mindset. They enjoy the challenge, and are always willing to work harder or try something different... as they are convinced their existing abilities can be enhanced or expanded as needed.

Now that we've compared and contrasted the two mindsets... it's pretty clear which one we must strive hard to have, right?

So, here are my top tips on **how to cultivate a growth mindset:**

1. Know that it's okay for things to go wrong. Just learn from it and move forward.

2. When you feel yourself getting emotional about a situation, walk away. Take some timeout to cool off, and then come back when you've cleared your mind and are ready to look at the situation logically.
3. Never be afraid to challenge yourself — you never know what you may discover you're capable of.
4. Don't limit yourself to what you know and believe today. Allow yourself to explore different thoughts and actions which may take you down a completely different road.
5. Recognise that effort, determination, and persistence eat talent for breakfast any day.
6. Consciously adopt a growth mindset and put it at the forefront of how you operate.
7. As Jim Rohn put it: "Don't wish it was easier; wish you were better. Don't wish for less problems; wish for more skills. And don't wish for less challenges; wish for more wisdom."

Many times on my journey as a Project Management Professional, I have found myself sitting with one of my team members… feeling like I was a counsellor. I would either try to help them solve a life crisis or provide them with career advice.

Strangely, I thought project delivery was all just about driving a team to deliver the agreed scope within budget to an agreed timeline. Well, let me tell you for a fact that 50% or more of your time revolves around people.

And when you're dealing with people, you're going to need fundamental soft skills such as:

- Critical Thinking
- Problem Solving
- Public Speaking & Mastering Communication for Influence
- Leadership Skills
- Teamwork
- Empathy
- Positivity
- Conflict Resolution & Negotiation Skills

Now, none of the formal training I have completed has ever provided me with the experience to apply these soft skills.

What did help me was cultivating a growth mindset that allowed me to effectively lead people... avoid or resolve conflicts with them... and ultimately have a harmonious working relationship with them.

That's why I firmly believe that adopting a growth mindset is one of the key areas of focus and skills that will help you build the qualities... that will propel your career as a Project Management Professional.

But it's not the only thing.

Key Areas of Focus and Skills for a Project Manager

Here are other key areas of focus and skills that will help you become the best Project Management Professional possible:

1 - Always Looking Ahead in Traffic

Do you remember the first thing you were taught when you were first learning to ride a bike?

Look straight ahead. Not at the pedal. Not at the ground. Not at your handlebars. Just look right where you're headed.

And when you were first learning how to drive a car, didn't you hear the same advice?

I bet you did.

And now that you're preparing for a career as a Project Management Professional, I'm repeating the same lesson... because it's an important one.

Just like when you're driving in traffic, you have to always see what's happening in front of you. Not for the fun of it... but to avoid any accidents. It's both a skill and a survival mechanism to keep looking ahead... so you could make reasonable predictions based on what you can see in foresight.

If you practise and master this skill, you will soon learn to pre-empt things that may go wrong when you're delivering a project. This could be a gamechanger when you are running complex projects.

2 - Communicating Effectively

Many times in my career, I fell victim to being too busy and driving results… so much so that I sometimes forgot to communicate critical messages to my team or stakeholders. This has gotten me in one too many sticky situations, which is why I don't want you making the same mistake.

Remember that communication is KING.

As such, you need to make it a pivotal element of how you manage projects. Whether it's good or bad news, you always have to communicate it to the applicable parties, be it your team members, vendors, stakeholders, sponsors, or executive leadership teams. Making sure everyone is in the know is a crucial leadership skill every Project Manager needs.

And speaking of leadership…

3 - Inspiring Others Through Leadership

Ever heard of entire teams leaving organisations… to follow their leader to wherever they're going next?

That's a testament to how great the leader is. If you can inspire people through great leadership… they will follow you to hell and back. Hopefully, they won't have to… but that is to say they will support you in everything you need to achieve.

This is why leadership is a skill worth focusing on… as it can have a significant impact on the productivity of your team, and, in effect, the success of your projects. Remember that no one will want to work — much less work hard — for a boss that's a certified a-hole.

So, it's high time you recognise that leadership and people skills are just as important as hard, technical skills. And as you work on developing your leadership skills… be sure to draw a hard line between leading and dictating.

Remember that leaders never dictate; rather, they inspire others to make the right choices. As former US President Ike Eisenhower would say: "Leadership is the art of getting someone else to do something you want done... because he/she wants to do it."

4 - Exhibiting Real Empathy

You don't want to be the kind of Project Manager who learns that someone had a death in the family and immediately goes: "But you're still coming to work on Monday, right?"

Everyone hates leaders who do that.

That's why you've got to have real empathy for the people around you. That includes your team members, vendors, and stakeholders. And to give real empathy to these people, you need to take the time to get to know them. Trust me — that's the only way you'd start caring for people authentically. You've got to form real relationships with those you work with, so you can become attuned to how they are feeling... what motivates them... and what grinds their gears.

And regardless of how hectic project delivery might get... you have to realise that work is not the only source of pressure and stress in people's lives. Be conscious of the fact that the people you're working with also have personal struggles they may be dealing with from time to time.

Now, this is not about you having to be all "touchy-feely" with your professional peers... but the old "walking a mile in another man's shoes" might be a great rule of thumb to follow when dealing with people.

5 - Identifying and Effectively Hedging Against Risks

Benjamin Franklin once said there are only two things certain in this world: death and taxes.

I hate to disagree with the guy... but I actually think there are three things certain in life:

Death, taxes, and risks.

As with most things in our lives, project delivery comes with a lot of risks, which, if not managed well, can leave any of us flat on our face.

That's why I've formed a habit to hold risk review sessions with my teams. And I don't only do it as part of the initial project planning, as important as that risk review session might be. What I do is hold weekly sessions to review new risks that may have bubbled up to the surface as we go along the project delivery journey. I do this to give my team enough time to hedge against those risks before it's too late.

Because while risks are inevitable with every project, you could eliminate and or manage most of those risks by identifying them on time.

6 - *Maintaining Your Integrity*

In 2007, Oprah Winfrey founded an all-girls school in South Africa. That same year, a dorm manager was accused of taking advantage of the students under their care.

It was a big scandal, for sure. But someone of Oprah Winfrey's background and statute could have easily swept things under the rug and walked away unscathed.

Instead, she took action by personally travelling to South Africa to resolve the crisis… hiring investigators… and recruiting a trauma specialist for students.

On top of all that, she openly spoke about the incident multiple times, including during a commencement speech she made to Stanford graduates in 2008.

And instead of blaming her for it, people respected her more for how she dealt with the situation.

That's the kind of leader I want you to be as you propel your career as a Project Management Professional.

When dealing with situations in the workplace that test your integrity… always act like everyone's watching. That may or may not be true. Nonetheless, it's important to always maintain integrity by being honest…

admitting your mistakes… treating everyone the same… and staying true to your commitments.

You need to remember that it is your actions, not your words, that set the tone for your team. And it is by "walking the talk" that you can earn the trust of others.

Remember that there is no shame in admitting when you've made a mistake. What matters more is how you strive to do better moving forward.

Take solace from the words of the one and only Michael Jordan:

"I've missed more than 9,000 shots in my career. I've lost almost 300 games. 26 times, I've been trusted to take the game winning shot and missed. I've failed over and over and over again in my life. And that is why I succeed."

And with that, I hope you take the time to understand and apply all the lessons presented in this chapter… whether you're an aspiring or seasoned project management professional. Because everything I've tried to impart here forms part of a surefire recipe not only to increase your value in the marketplace… but also to open yourself up to more diverse opportunities as you master this wonderful craft.

CHAPTER 8

Stuff They Don't Teach in Schools

Youth is truly wasted on the young.

As a kid, I had this sort of love-hate relationship with school.

On one hand, I did enjoy the process of learning, and even more so the opportunity to make friends and be around my peers! Back then, making new friends didn't feel as difficult as it does now. In fact, it was easy. The social aspect that school gives children is just difficult to beat... and near impossible to replicate in adulthood. Those 15 minutes before the school bell went, recess, lunch breaks, and then the couple of hours after the final bell went... those played host to some of my fondest childhood memories.

But on the other hand, all the other parts of school felt like something I had no choice but to tolerate in exchange for all the fun parts. Kind of like having to eat your vegetables in order to get dessert. I remember the largely robotic experience of getting up, showering, having breakfast, getting changed, and heading to school for the day... and then heading home for dinner, homework and some playtime, until it's time to head off to bed and prepare to do it all again the next day.

Despite this love-hate relationship, though, I stuck with it. I sat there, day after day, learning how to pick up and digest information in the most efficient way... so that I could apply those learnings to real-life problems and challenges in the future.

And I didn't stop there.

As a young IT professional and later as a project manager, I went out and got my hands on every certification I could get... once again thinking the routinary, robotic world of formal education was something I needed to tolerate to equip myself for a professional career.

Ah, if only I knew then what I know now...

Perhaps I could have avoided so much pain and suffering... while making a lot more progress in my career.

See, I thought the whole point of school was to absorb every bit of content and information the teachers and instructors gave me. And I thought that's all I needed to take in to prepare myself for the 'real world.'

But I thought wrong. Like I said... youth is wasted on the young.

What I realised later than I should have, was that at the end of the day, schools exist to try and help you land a job. And that's all well and good. But when you do land that job and you start to face real clients with real problems... you won't be able to solely rely on what you've learned in school.

And if what you learned in school is all you've got... then you could run into big trouble.

I know I did.

Let me tell you that story.

The Role of Formal Education in Becoming a Successful Project Manager

Some time ago, when working in IT, I was asked to kick off a Cyber Security project. It wasn't an overly difficult project per se, but the timeline the client wanted made me feel like I was looking down the barrel of a gun.

I found myself sitting in front of our customer telling me:

"I don't care how you do it, Leo, but this project needs to be delivered by the end of April."

And guess what?

It was already the 1st of March that day.

I felt the blood rush from the rest of my body and into my head… as my brain went into overdrive, thinking how I could respond professionally and politely.

All I could come up with was:

"If delivering this project is possible by the end of April, then we will definitely do this for you."

Thinking back, it wasn't anywhere near the right response… Lol.

I should have leveraged the science of the project plan my team and I meticulously prepared to explain the situation to the customer. I should have found the right words to explain politely to the client that the timeline they're asking for is virtually impossible to meet.

But the fact of the matter was that it was just my third day on the job working for this IT Managed Service Provider… and they had just told me that morning that I had a project kickoff for an important client they wanted me to run.

That meant I had yet to do any planning or even understand the full scope of the project… and I was like a deer in headlights the whole time.

At the time, I felt like all the years I'd spent in school and post-graduate training amounted to nothing. I felt like all my degrees, diplomas, certifications, and credentials betrayed me… and left me high and dry.

And it was then that I realised I had landed myself in a brand new school.

Some call it the University of Life. Others call it the School of Hard Knocks.

But whatever you want to call it… one thing is for sure. This was the school where you learn everything they didn't teach you in every other school you've attended before.

Because like I told you earlier… all my formal education and academic training failed to help me when I was sitting in front of the client, getting pressured to agree to a deadline I knew was impossible to achieve.

That meant I had a lot of stuff I had yet to learn... that they just didn't teach me in school.

Now, does that mean formal education is practically useless?

Of course not.

Academic learning has given me the foundations of learning. It was because of school that I know how to take in information critically, so that I may improve on it before I use it in any real-life scenarios. It was that process of learning how to learn that I truly enjoyed, and for that I am still grateful for the years I spent getting formal education.

And besides, school qualifications are very, very good at providing you with the hard skills you need in order to do your job completely. After all, intelligence is a pretty good predictor of success in that way. For instance, your ability to solve a complex logic problem, which is assessed through IQ tests, is reflective of a person's ability to solve a complex engineering, legal, or project management problem.

But at the end of the day, Jim Rohn was right when he said:

"Formal education will make you a living, but self-education will make you a fortune."

The Stuff They Don't Teach in Schools

You see, the University of Life and the School of Hard Knocks is also known by another name:

The School of Self Education and Personal Development.

As you go through life as a Project Management Professional, you'd find many different opportunities to develop and self-educate... whether intentionally or by being forced through difficult situations.

And that's how you learn about the stuff they don't teach any of us in school.

But waiting until your back is against the wall just to learn important life lessons... is not at all a pleasant experience.

So, to at least lessen the things you have to learn the hard way... let me share with you some of the things I've learned on my journey through life... both from a personal and professional perspective.

Think of this as a free prep course before you enrol yourself in The School of Self Education and Personal Development.

Now, here are six things they don't teach us in academia... but are nevertheless crucial in surviving and thriving as a Project Management Professional... and as a holistic individual:

Lesson #1: Communication, Communication, Communication

American author Simon Sinek was right on the money when he explained why many adult professionals have stunted communication skills.

Sinek explained that up until adolescence, the most important approval for us is the approval of our parents. But once we hit that age of adolescence, our priorities start to change. Suddenly, we no longer care what our parents say or think about us. Because the most important approval we can get at this point is that of our peers. So, we pick up communication skills trying to deal with our adolescent peer groups.

We learn how to communicate to resolve conflicts among friends, to protect our reputations, and ultimately, to get people to like us.

But isn't it concerning how most of that is actually self-taught?

Sure, we do have language classes in school, but those were reserved for learning the rules of grammar and speech... and not the rules of effective communication... especially in times of crisis.

And who's to say the communication skills we taught ourselves when dealing with our peers are applicable to a professional setting? I mean... could you imagine talking to a client the same way you talk to your friends? That would be disastrous!

This is why many adults and professionals lack advanced communication skills. Because we don't learn effective communication from school... we only go by the communication skills we picked up from talking and dealing with our friends. And as we've established, those skills are just not advanced enough for all the communicating we need to do as professionals.

So, to help you gain this very crucial skill that they don't teach us in school... here are the four communication principles I live and swear by:

#1. Say It More Than Once

Never assume that people have understood what you have told them... especially if it was their first time hearing it.

As frustrating as it may be for some of us, repetition is going to be and has always been the key to communicating effectively. So, when it comes to working in the corporate world, be patient enough to repeat yourself to make sure that the person you're talking to completely understands the message you're trying to get across. Don't be like parents who tell their kids in trouble: *"Don't make me repeat myself... again!"*

I mean, I know when I manage projects, programs, or deal with key stakeholders... I continually repeat myself as I plant the "seed of understanding" into their minds for important things I need them to understand. After all, I'd rather be known as the person who always repeats myself... rather than the person who is always misunderstood.

#2: Pay Attention to Nonverbal Communication

It's pretty easy to understand what another person is saying. But the ability to understand what they're *not* saying is a very powerful skill that puts you ahead of the pack.

So, strive to understand human interactions at a deeper level by paying attention to nonverbal communication. After all, most experts agree that 70 to 93% of all communication is nonverbal. That includes nonverbal communication cues such as eye contact, voice patterns, and body language. This is one area which might be worth learning more about for you... especially if you are managing or leading teams.

#3: Listen

I'm sure you've heard this one before...

But aren't you curious why we as people are designed with two ears and just one mouth? Seems like a pretty obvious hint that we should listen twice as much as we speak, no?

See, I've learned from the many conflicts I have found myself in with regards to my personal and professional relationships... that it's not only important to learn how to speak well. In fact, it may even be more important to master the flip side of the coin — which is to listen well.

And remember — listening is not the same as hearing. Hearing refers to sound hitting our ears... and it happens to us as a subconscious physical process. On the other hand, listening requires your focus and concentration to take place. It actually means being aware of both verbal and nonverbal communication elements... which then allows you to truly understand what is being told to you.

Here's the problem with many of us. When someone talks to us, we listen to counter. We listen to respond. At times, we even retort before having allowed the other person to finish what they're saying.

What we should be doing instead is engaging in active listening. That means showing genuine interest and concentrating on what the other person is saying when they're speaking to us. This encourages the other person to communicate fully, openly, and honestly.

#4. Keep It Simple.

We all know the saying:

"If you can't dazzle them with brilliance, then baffle them with bull."

Well, that's not what I mean when I say keep your communication simple. Of course, you want to make sure the communication you use is relevant or at the level of the person you're talking to.

It serves no purpose, unless you're at a job interview, to try and look good by grandstanding... when all you want to do is get a message across to someone.

Personally, I guide my communication with two simple questions:

First: "What's in it for them?"

If what I want to say is neither relevant nor beneficial to the other person, I don't say it. That's one way I keep things simple.

Now, the second question: "Would a 10-year-old be able to understand what I am saying?"

This guide question has served me well in using clear and simple language when communicating with someone. It has allowed me to remove EGO from the communication experience... and instead make it all about the person I'm trying to communicate with.

Again, the purpose of all the communication you'd be making as a Project Management Professional is not to impress or bedazzle anyone... but for the person you're talking to... to walk away with a clear understanding of what it is that you need them to know, understand, or do.

Lesson #2: Fail Fast, Don't Avoid It

Thomas Watson, the late chairman and CEO of IBM, was once asked what he planned to do to an employee who made a mistake that cost his company $600,000.

People wanted to know if he'd fire the employee... but this is what he had to say:

"I just spent $600,000 training him."

It just goes to show that some of the world's most successful people think of mistakes — or failures — as training.

And I agree with that.

117

Most of us spend a lifetime trying to avoid failure. And it is precisely because of that approach to life... that many of us don't live life to the fullest.

But wouldn't you agree that getting things wrong is an important part of the learning process?

I remember one huge mistake I made when I was still an apprentice ground engineer with Qantas. I was performing a regular service oil change on an ancillary pump in a jumbo jet engine. In training, I learned from reading the maintenance procedure that I needed to depressurise the pump before changing the oil.

But guess what?

That's exactly what I forgot to do when I was performing the oil change! So, as soon as I removed the oil drain plug, I ended up with a face full of oil. Luckily, I didn't forget to have my eye protection goggles on!

Now, did I fail in this maintenance procedure execution?

Miserably.

But did I ever forget to depressurise the pump before changing the oil again?

Never.

Never again.

I've learned my lesson from that one mistake.

See? We will face many failures in our lives. After all, nobody's perfect. What's important is how we deal with each failure and mistake... and how we grow from them. But let me tell you that growth would never take place if you limit the way you live life... in order to avoid failures.

So, I highly suggest that you accept, as early as now, that it's impossible to avoid failure. And unless you're planning to stop living, embrace it as part of the process for learning... and don't try to avoid it at all costs.

And whatever you do, don't fail for lack of trying. Or lack of willingness to take risks.

Aspire to be better than the millions of people who quit before they succeed — just because they encountered some roadblocks at the start of their journey.

Fail often and fail fast, if that's what it takes for you to learn, wise up, and never make the same mistakes again.

And if it helps, remember that Thomas Alva Edison didn't invent the incandescent light bulb on the first try. Keep in mind that people were already mocking him for failing thousands of times, but he just kept on trying. And he got rewarded in the end for it.

How? Well, when people were making fun of him for "failing," he simply said:

"I have not failed; I've just found 10,000 ways that won't work."

Lesson #3: Manage your Finances

Here's another great quote you may or may not have heard before:

"Beware of little expenses; a small leak will sink a great ship." - Benjamin Franklin

Hey, look, I'm not a finance expert. But I have gotten myself out of living pay cheque to pay cheque — and I've got some tips to share with you on how to do the same.

Now, let me start with another disclaimer.

I never used to look at my finances, outside of confirming that a pay cheque had come into my bank account… and that I wasn't going to run out of money. Ultimately, my activities would be determined by what I had in my bank account. Some days I'd be like: "Well, looks like it's peanut butter on Arnott's SAO biscuits tonight" as I'm waiting for that next pay cheque to arrive.

Again, this comes as no surprise with schools still refusing to teach us how to manage our personal finances.

And for some reason, as Project Management Professionals... we seem to be familiar with various techniques to manage project budgets... but when it comes to personal finances, we are quite literally trumped!

This just begs the question...

Why are we released to the world with almost no financial education?

So, I want to share some of the simple but invaluable tips and principles I have learnt and still use today to avoid living pay cheque to pay cheque:

#1. Just because you make a dollar, doesn't mean you have to spend a dollar.

Nothing's wrong with enjoying the fruits of your labour... but it's not okay to always spend everything you earn! I know that with marketing all around us and in our pockets (i.e. mobile phones) 24/7, it's getting increasingly hard to stay away from that BUY NOW button in every ad on Facebook.

But to be quite frank, all you need as a starting point is common sense... and managing that consumer mindset that urges you to buy something all the time.

When I personally adopted this mindset of second-guessing that little voice inside my head that says:

"You deserve to buy this..."

I suddenly always found myself with money in the bank and in my wallet!

#2. Live below your means

I apologise for stating the obvious...

But if this one were truly *that* obvious... do you think people would still have ballooning credit card debts? I'm speaking from experience here, as someone who, at one point, had lost control of his credit card spending... that it started controlling me! I was in so much stress and suffering... and I wouldn't wish that feeling on my worst enemy!

So, let me repeat this to you, as obvious as it may seem:

Live below your means.

Do not spend more than you actually earn.

And if you have credit cards, don't think of them as extra money. Just take advantage of interest-free staggered payments and afterpay… but do not swipe them on things you can't actually afford from what you earn!

When I started consciously living on less than what I actually earned… the financial stress I used to experience became a total thing of the past for me.

#3. Save 10-15% of What You Make

This tip is life-changing.

And the funny thing is that most of us have heard about this… but very few actually do it.

Personally, I have experienced what it's like to live pay cheque to pay cheque. At the time, I was oblivious to any other way. So, although I did not enjoy that lifestyle, I accepted that this was just how things were.

I remember some 20 years ago as I started my own personal development journey… I was told by one of my coaches about the concept of saving 10-15% of what you make and was recommended to read that great book you may have heard of called "The Richest Man In Babylon" by George S Clason. It's a book which changed my perspective on saving.

Then, I was told to extract this amount of money from my pay before I start to spend any of it.

Thank heavens I had the good sense to listen to that advice when I heard it. Now, saving 15% of what I make is something I have been doing for years… and it has given me the freedom to weather tough times as needed financially. That's why I highly recommend this as part of building your financial muscle.

#4. Build Your Emergency & Travel Fund

This is yet another basic advice that many have heard… but few have followed.

So, let me reiterate to you that building an emergency fund is very important.

I know for me and my wife, Tiffany, we have plans of travelling around Australia for 6-12 months in the near future.

121

This means we formally won't be exchanging time or value for money... as a way of living during that time. We'd simply be absorbing all elements of being on holiday... and reaping the rewards of our hard work for a period of time.

And how are we able to do this?

Well, we have our emergency fund for that! We've saved six months worth of our living costs... and that's what we'll use to fund our trip.

After that trip, we'd once again build up that fund for any other holiday we'd like to take... or any emergency situation we'd have to spend on in the future.

This way, we always have that extra money to pull out... without having to rely on our pay cheques for emergency or holiday expenses.

Having said that, let me close this topic of managing your personal finances... with this highly sensible quote from Robert Kiyosaki:

"It's not how much money you make, but how much money you keep, how hard it works for you, and how many generations you keep it for."

Lesson #4: Are you the Alien? Dare to be Different

"To thine own self be true."

These are words written by William Shakespeare centuries ago... but still hold great value to this day.

See, ultimately, I believe we are all aliens.

As early as elementary school, I already knew I was not like the others.

I would unwrap my home-made, tea towel-wrapped lunch and to pull out what's known today as "Pane Di Casa." Those are hand-cut, 4cm-thick slices of bread which I had with veal schnitzel, lettuce, and tomatoes.

As I finished my first bite, I would have flour dust all over my face… all the way down the front of my school shirt. I remember feeling silly and embarrassed in front of the other kids as they stared at the sandwich I was eating… that was almost as big as my head.

Today, these gourmet sandwiches are considered a luxury in Sydney CBD where office workers would go out for lunch to get themselves the biggest and tastiest food options… to satisfy their lunchtime hunger before heading back to the office.

Some would say I was just ahead of my time.

The reality is…

Many of us live life trying to be like others, be it at work or in school. We are terrified to be different, lest we be deemed as aliens. Of course, it doesn't help that societal standards have preconceived notions of what we should look like… what we should eat… what we should say… and what we should do.

And in trying to fit into those societal standards and norms… we regularly shed the wonderful things about ourselves that make us UNIQUE in this world. I see this often when interviewing job applicants. I'd ask them about their attributes that make them perfect for the role they're applying for… and people nearly always miss mentioning the most unique, eccentric, and special things about them.

I guess no one was taught about Coco Chanel in school, and how she once said:

"In order to be irreplaceable, one must always be different."

See, one of the best things you can do in this life… is to embrace who you are in all its glory. Be it the colour of your skin… the clothes you wear… your nationality… or the food you eat.

Dare to be an ALIEN.

I know we all tried so hard to fit in when we were young… but I have long dismissed that urge. Today, I believe feeling like an alien when I'm surrounded by the masses is one of the best feelings in the world. In fact, I feel most confident when I know I'm not trying to blend in… and instead standing out in the midst of conformists.

To be a great project manager, you've got to be irreplaceable. And what did Coco Chanel say about being irreplaceable again? Oh, right — you've got to be different. After all, you need to talk and act a certain way when you're talking to clients, partners, and even your team members. So, why not just talk and act as YOU... and allow your true, unique self to drive your results for you? Why go to the trouble of becoming something you're not... when it's a lot easier to just be true to yourself?

Well, I guess it's hard to unlearn things you've learned from your youth... so here are a few tips on how you can make your unique self shine through now:

- Acknowledge and accept that humanity thrives through diversity. Being different is actually the norm... not the anomaly. So, don't you dare cut out the most amazing parts about yourself just to fit the cookie cutter kind of person society expects you to be.
- Learn to love and accept yourself. Trust that it makes all the difference. Start by acknowledging the things that make you different... whether or not you actually like those things about yourself. Then, instead of keeping them hidden from the world, work on bringing them out in a way that allows you to slowly embrace who you are.

  But be warned that not everyone will like and accept the real you. That's why the people you surround yourself with also play a significant part in this process of self-love and self-acceptance. The support they provide and the encouragement they give you will make this process a lot easier. So, as Les Brown would say – "surround yourself with quality people only". Make sure you surround yourself with people who will encourage you, and not discourage you, from being YOU.

- Simply accept that we can't please everyone. There's no reason to allow our lives to be directed by other people's expectations instead of our own.

  I remember when I used to try and please everyone. Sure, I made other people happy. But ultimately, for me, it became a tiresome cycle hiding behind a mask. I figured I'd just stay true to myself, whatever happens. And true enough, I lost some people in that process. But the people who mattered the most didn't mind. They celebrated me in my truest, most authentic form, and I can tell you there's no better feeling in the world.

Lesson #5: People Power - Build your Life Family

I have gone through life depending on the one person that always has my best interests at heart… and supports me under all circumstances — ME!

In running an IT Support & Consulting Business, I learned to understand the power of people in a collective… especially when they're aligned to a common cause or outcome.

When people come together as a team to support each other in delivering an outcome, be it a project, an assignment or otherwise, they become very powerful.

Think of a solo athlete. Let's say an F1 racer. On the surface, it might look like they are operating alone. After all, each vehicle only has one person driving it. He's the one who's got to train, be in condition, and perform well on the day of the race. But if you know what exactly happens on that track… you know that F1 racers are never working alone. They've got mentors, coaches, and every single person in their pit crews all working hard to ensure their victory.

The same is true for us Project Management Professionals. After all, behind many a great and successful manager is what I call PEOPLE POWER. These are the QUALITY PEOPLE who become your LIFE support. The people who lift you up when you're feeling down… who help you find a way forward when you think all options have been exhausted… and more importantly, who believe in you when you think you have nothing more to give. In other words, this is your life family.

I've had many days, weeks and months, when I ran my business feeling hopeless and ready to throw in the towel. But what I discovered was that I was never alone… and did not have to run the business on my own. In fact, I had a multitude of people around me who were willing to help and support me, if only I let them.

So, let me ask you this:

When was the last time you leveraged the PEOPLE POWER around you?

And, more importantly, do you know how to?

See, learning to accept help when you need it, is critical to your wellbeing. But it's something that many of us do not understand… since it is neither taught in schools or at home. Instead, we were largely taught to *always* be independent and depend on our own strengths all the time.

But hey, no man is an island, right?

In reality, you have your team of project delivery professionals to provide you with People Power. Remember that these people you work with are not just there so you could have people to delegate tasks to. They're also there to give you encouragement, advice, and support for your overall personal growth.

As they say… the whole is always greater than the sum of its parts.

And I have learnt that to live a long and happy life as a Project Manager… you've got to firmly believe that "together, everyone achieves MORE!"

Project Managers Movement (PMM), is a safe, non-judgmental community that encourages Project Delivery Professionals… corporate leaders… and employees… to share knowledge, support each other, build lifelong authentic friendships as we acknowledge our individual uniqueness while focusing on our own self-mastery through both personal & professional development… and was born through a dream I have had for over 10 years.

But I never would have been able to build it beyond inception… without the help of my Spiritual Coach, Phuong Phan… who awakened a conscious awareness in me that allowed me to bend what I thought was my reality at the time. Because I was able to leverage the People Power that Coach Phan extended to me, PMM became a reality.

And not only that.

PMM has now become a source of inspiration, support, and encouragement for many professionals like myself. It has thus become my calling to bring together incredible individuals who know they have more to learn about themselves… and even more to share with others as part of a global family that embraces and understands the importance of People Power.

But do note that People Power and the concept of building your life family is not just limited to the work setting. Your life family could also include family, friends, neighbours, acquaintances, social groups, professional networks, and even the friends of your friends. All these people have the potential to be part of your life family… by providing you with People Power when you need it.

So, while I know that you can be independent and self-sustaining… do not ignore the extra boost People Power can bring to your life and career. I know learning how to build my life family and leveraging the People Power they willingly gave me… transformed my life, and will continue to forever.

As Hellen Keller would love to remind us:

"Alone we can do so little; together we can do so much."

Lesson #6: Make Decisions Quickly

Decisions, decisions, decisions.

Did you know we make about 35,000 of those in a day?

Crazy, right?

35,000 thousand or so decisions… and only 24 hours in which to try and make the best ones. It's truly insane… especially if you think about the fact that the quality of our lives ultimately depends on the decisions we make day by day.

So, again, it just begs the question:

All those years we spent in school… why wasn't a single day spent teaching us how to make the best, most beneficial decisions in the fastest way possible?

Well, at least we have Malcolm Gladwell, right? In his book *Blink: The Power of Thinking Without Thinking...* Gladwell taught us that the best decisions we make in life are the ones we make in a snap.

And I am inclined to agree.

Just looking at the math suggests that most of our decisions have to be made in a snap... or we risk stagnation. Again, we have 35,000 decisions to make in a span of 24 hours. If you can't even decide what to eat for breakfast or what to wear for your morning meeting in less than a minute... you'd be in big trouble!

This is exactly why some of the world's richest (and busiest) businessmen have completely rejected fashion... and simply wear the same thing every single day. Think Steve Jobs and his iconic black-shirt-and-jeans outfit. He had dozens of the same pieces of clothing in his wardrobe... so that he could eliminate having to wake up and decide on what to wear. He believed that reducing the number of decisions he had to make even by just one... would make him more productive and more capable of making better decisions where it mattered the most.

Perhaps that's what I should have done in 1992, when my sister decided to move with her family to Queensland.

See, it was a great time back then and the property market was not what it is today. So, my sister managed to pick up this incredible hilltop property of over 10 acres within an area which had just then been developed.

As a young man back then, I had mum and dad asking me when I was going to buy a property myself... and to be honest, it was the furthest thing from my mind!

But then I started thinking about it...

On one hand, I knew that in the same area where my sister brought her property, newly subdivided blocks were on sale for less than $150K. And that was a lot of money for me back then. But the flip side of the coin was that the market back then was hot. It was a buyers' market, actually. It would have been the most ideal time for me to buy.

So, I thought about it some more. And then some more.

And before I knew it, 15 years had passed. The area got massively developed... and of course, prices skyrocketed! I sat on it for 15 years, and ended up with a lot of regret... as I could no longer afford to buy the property even if I wanted to.

I just can't stress this enough — youth is truly wasted on the young!

Now, one of my most powerful learnings as a business owner and leader is around making quick yet good decisions. A bit of emphasis on quick, though, because learning to make better decisions ultimately requires the act of making the decision... before you run out of options.

You've experienced this, right? How great leaders have the ability to make decisions in an instant... while the other, more inexperienced members of the team are still stuck in analysis paralysis mode? That's a mark of an effective leader.

So, let me give you a few tips based on my own experiences with making tough decisions in a snap. Hopefully, these tips will encourage you to embrace situations where you have to make a choice... and decide on one thing before a decision is made for you:

- When you find yourself in a position where your emotional state is high, try and avoid making BIG decisions. As with all decision-making, you need to carefully weigh the pros and cons of your decision... and that requires a logical and mostly unemotional state of mind from you. Otherwise, you won't be able to identify the best way to move forward. An example of this is when you have a heated argument with your partner. If you don't wait until you have calmed down before making any decisions... you may unintentionally decide to say or do something that you might regret. And the worst part is that you might not be able to take any of it back!

- I know I said it's important for you to learn how to make decisions in a snap. Nevertheless, some decisions are more important than others, and must not be rushed. The real skill, therefore, is identifying situations where you have to make an instant decision... and distinguishing them from situations where you need to step back and think first. When faced with a big decision that does not have to be made on the spot... it is crucial to allow yourself the time to digest and maybe sleep on it... until such time that you actually have to make the decision.

- One of the things I always reminded myself of is the fact that many other people have likely made the same decisions that I am trying to make. Especially in the context of Project Management... it sometimes makes sense to do some research about similar decisions other Project Management Professionals have made in the past...

that relate to the situation you find yourself in. Even if you end up going a different direction… knowing how other people navigated the same dilemmas could give you an insight on what outcomes have resulted from those decisions.

And that completes my personal list of things that school didn't teach us… but should have.

Now, I encourage you to question your own education… and try to find gaps in what you've learned through formal education. Perhaps, you could come up with your own list of things that you wish you had been taught at school… and perhaps you could take it upon yourself to learn those things yourself in your quest towards personal development and self-learning.

Start Self-Learning

All of us have been born into a world that tries to limit how we think and live.

But you don't have to allow the world around you to limit your potential as a person… and as a Project Management Professional.

Go beyond what you've been taught and discover new ways of thinking, acting, and decision-making.

Hopefully, this chapter has given you a great vantage point to start your own journey towards personal development and self-learning.

Not many people would be keen on pushing past the limits of their comfort zones… but by now you already know that some of the best things this life has to offer… exist outside of what you currently know and believe in.

So, keep on questioning what you've been taught, even if it makes you feel different from others. Remember our discussion on how it's okay to feel like an alien?

It's just like what Les Brown said:

"You must be willing to do what others won't do, to have what others won't have."

And in this case, what you could end up having... is an extraordinary career as a great Project Management Professional.

I can't wait to find out what lessons you'll end up teaching yourself and passing on to others... as you continue on this journey!

CHAPTER 9

Be The Eagle Not the Chicken

Story time!

Picture an eagle's nest in the mountainside with four large eagle eggs inside.

One day, an earthquake rocked the mountain, causing one of the eggs to roll down the mountain and straight into a chicken farm located in the valley below.

When the chickens saw the egg, it felt instinctive for them to protect and care for the eagle egg. Eventually, the eagle egg hatched, and a beautiful baby eagle was born.

But obviously, the chickens raised the eagle as one of them. That's why the eagle grew up believing he was nothing more than a chicken. The eagle did what the other chickens did. It scratched in the dirt for seeds. It clucked and crackled. And it never flew more than a few feet above ground because none of the other chickens did.

The eagle loved his home and family, but it seemed his spirit cried out for more.

One day, the eagle looked to the skies above and noticed a group of mighty eagles soaring.

"Oh," the eagle cried, "I wish I could soar like those birds."

The chickens roared with laughter.

"You cannot soar like those eagles. You are a chicken and chickens do not soar."

But the little eagle continued staring at the eagles above, dreaming that he could one day be like them.

One day, while playing a game on the farm, the eagle again looked to the skies above and noticed an eagle soaring gracefully and majestically in the skies.

He again asked the chickens:

"What is that beautiful bird?"

The chickens replied, "That is an eagle. He is an outstanding bird, but you cannot fly like him because you are just a chicken."

So, the eagle never gave it a second thought, believing that to be truth.

He lived the life of, and died as, a chicken depriving himself of his heritage and never knowing the grand life that could have been his.

Feel bad for the baby eagle?

Well, the truth is, many of us are just like the eagle... stuck living its life as a chicken.

Remember, more than 100 years ago, it was considered impossible to run the mile in under four minutes.

Did we have evidence that it wasn't possible?

No, of course not.

We just didn't have proof that it *could* be done... and so we dismissed it as impossible.

Just like we didn't have proof that a person could summit all 14 of the world's 8,000-metre peaks in a year's time... which is why for many many years, people thought it to be impossible.

No one actually did a mathematical calculation of the fastest a human can travel. No one checked the maximum oxygen capacity of a healthy person. No one accounted for the specific effects fatigue is going to have on an otherwise fit physique.

No one went through all of that meticulous data-gathering to work out... whether or not hitting all 14 peaks in a year is scientifically, humanly possible.

For the most part, people have just looked at the mountains and said:

Gee, that looks difficult. In fact, it's so difficult, I'm going to use the word 'impossible' to describe it.

Until Nepali mountaineer Nimsdai Purja proved us all misguided.

In the film 14 Peaks: Nothing is Impossible, we all saw how Nimsdai, along with a skilled team of Sherpas, took on the seemingly insurmountable task of reaching 14 summits in less than a year… and did it in a record time of under seven months.

This just proves that all our limiting beliefs on what is possible and what is not… may not truly be accurate.

It's not that your wildest dreams are impossible.

It's just that no one has dared to try.

And until someone does, we'd all be like the baby eagle who was raised by chickens… thinking he could never soar as high.

Personal & Professional Dissonance

Have you ever felt like there was something more meant for you in life?

Perhaps you've woken up one morning, and while following the same routine you do every day, something inside you stirs and you start dreaming about all the possibilities. Until all of a sudden, the kids run into the kitchen… and thoughts of the day ahead replace your optimistic daydreaming.

Well, I myself have found that there are many great forces that surround us in life. Just like the waves at the beach trying to push you back to shore… there are energy forces that play on our minds and direct the actions we take each day… that sometimes either hold us right where we are… or have us line up, waiting for our turn to step up.

The Cognitive Dissonance Theory suggests that all of us have this inner drive holding all our attitudes and behaviours in harmony… in order to avoid chaos and dissonance. This is known as the principle of cognitive consistency.

Perhaps, that nagging feeling inside of you that you're meant for something more… is actually telling you that your actions and behaviours are not in alignment with what you actually believe in. Maybe it's trying to tell you that you're not supposed to be digging dirt, but soaring high.

So, ask yourself: what's holding you back from listening to that inner voice?

Could it be that you have a band of chickens around you telling you that you can't soar high like an eagle… because they'd like you to keep believing that you are nothing but a chicken?

Because that has happened to me in the past.

For a brief period when I was a young adult, I felt a deep yearning for belongingness. Although I've always felt like I was built differently from my peers… I couldn't shake the feeling of wanting to belong… both in my personal, social circles… and professionally.

For this reason, I remember almost losing my own identity in exchange for the kind of person my "friends" wanted me to be… or the kind of person my career needed me to be.

Thankfully, I found my way back to my own, true self. Otherwise, I never would have grown as an individual… as I would have just kept on adapting and camouflaging my true colours based on what pleased the people around me. And for that, I couldn't be grateful enough for that nagging voice inside me that kept on reminding me: *"This is not you."*

So, do you find yourself going around in circles, sometimes ending up right where you started… due to the influence of both your friends and the professional company you keep?

Let's be honest with each other for a moment.

Back when I was a ground engineer, all I did was go in the direction I was told to go. I followed the people around me, taking their advice without thinking if the same advice was helping me move forward… or holding me back. I was young and had no idea what I could become… outside of what other people told me I could be. If I had continued on down that path, I would have lost sight of the right path forward for me.

This is a pretty common scenario for young adults. And while there is nothing wrong in trying to learn and get guidance from the people around you... there should also be a conscious effort on your part to explore your own ideas, dreams, and visions for yourself!

At the same time, you must protect your own journey by making sure the people around you are helping you move upwards and onwards... instead of stunting your growth.

So, ask yourself this:

Are the people you spend most of your time with:

- Keeping you where you are
- Redirecting you from what you can see yourself achieving; and
- Influencing your direction based on their own fear and failures?

Or, are they encouraging you to discover what you're good at... by supporting what you want to do in life?

If it's anything other than the latter... that only means one thing:

There must be an eagle inside of you waiting to be discovered... and waiting to be heard through the noise of all the chickens clawing and cucking around you.

And in that case, you know what to do:

Find and release that eagle within.

How to Find the Eagle Within

Now, the first question you need to ask is:

What does it even mean to be an eagle?

And to help you answer that question... let me share with you some basic principles I've learned in my own personal quest to find and release the eagle within. These same principles could help you live the eagle's way of life... both in your personal and professional life:

1 - Alone BUT Together!

My decision to shift career paths from being an Aircraft Ground Engineer and moving into IT created a very interesting time in my life. My whole family couldn't understand why I'd leave behind a great career in aviation for something else!

And to tell you honestly, their doubts rubbed off on me. I started to double-guess my own decision, but in the end… my inner calling to do greater things became far too loud to ignore. In fact, it drowned out all the questioning voices around me… and I ended up knowing exactly what I needed to do:

That was to follow my own dreams… even if it meant having to fly solo… and away from the people who would rather see me stay where I was.

But here's what I found out about disconnecting from a crowd:

It doesn't last forever.

After all, we are inherently social beings.

That means it's only a matter of time before you stumble upon a new tribe that's ready to take you in. True enough, I did discover a new "crowd" along the way. I found people who were also trying to make changes in their lives and careers… most of whom also failed to gain the unwavering support of the people around them.

My point?

Being brave enough to walk the path alone when you need to is a great way to find success and personal fulfilment.

And this is one thing eagles are masters at.

They are comfortable flying alone… until they find their own kind to fly with. Even though there's no other eagle in sight for miles and miles… you'd never see an eagle flying with doves or chickens. That's because they don't have an issue with setting out alone. They keep on soaring and flying at the height and speed they're comfortable with… even if it means flying solo for days on end.

Remember this when you feel like the people around you do not support your personal visions and dreams. Because not everyone will. And the worst part is that other people's negativity and doubt could influence your own decisions — if you're not careful.

That's what makes it so critical that you don't waste your time with negative people. Instead, surround yourself with people who encourage you to follow your passion and dreams. And if you can't find such people... don't be afraid. The road less travelled may be lonely... but the worn-out path that everyone takes has much less delightful sights to offer.

So, be comfortable with the feeling of doing extraordinary things alone in your own unique way... because who knows what sorts of treasures you'd find along the way!

2 - *Always Focusing Ahead*

One of the most beautiful moments in life is living as a young adult — carefree, debt-free, and happy! At that point in life, it would seem as if the world is your oyster... and there's always something to look forward to in the road up ahead. That's why young adults are always so intense in seizing the day... and making the most of what they've got.

But once you progress to being a professional... a whole other world starts to appear. See, working in the corporate world can be both rewarding and enjoyable. But it can also be highly suffocating. The strict rules and power dynamics that exist in the workplace can put a damper on your spirit... and suddenly the world doesn't feel yours for the taking anymore. And so, you start to lose some of that intensity you used to have as a young adult.

This is especially true when we are "pigeon holed" into roles that dictate our authority, level of accountability, and the scope of work we could do for an organisation.

For someone like me who had entrepreneurial aspirations... working in such an environment felt like a trap. That's because my mind was constantly on the lookout for opportunities to get excited and ways to challenge the norm. As such, I often felt unfulfilled as a corporate worker.

But what bewildered me was the fact that I seemed to be alone in feeling that way. Many of the long-term employees I encountered... had fully succumbed to their destiny of being pigeon-holed in their roles... for the rest of their working life! They rarely even looked out the window!

Imagine that.

Imagine not seeing anything MORE for yourself and believing that your current situation is just how life will always be.

Well, my curse or blessing — you decide — was that my 'fruit for existence' was variety, learning, opportunity and connecting with so many different people.

That's why I could never be content doing the same every single day.

To this day, I still have the habit of asking the people I interact with... about what plans they have for themselves. Many tell me that they are WAITING to be placed on courses by their employer, so they are basically in a holding pattern.

Can you believe that... WAITING!

As if they have no personal vision for themselves... which they can use to pull themselves forward.

I know my life today was driven by my own appetite for focusing on what's up ahead... instead of getting stuck in the place I was at.

This is yet another eagle-like quality you'd want to cultivate in yourself.

That incredible vision and laser-sharp concentration when eagles prepare to swoop down on their prey — it gives them so much power. When they reach that point of focus and intense determination... pretty much nothing can stop them.

If you could learn to apply the same focus and intensity on your goals, aspirations, and dreams... you won't lose your way. No matter how hard the world and society around you might try to keep you blissfully stuck where you are... you'd always have that drive to dream higher, and achieve bigger things in life.

And if you could harness your vision to consciously keep track of what's waiting for you up ahead... you won't be blinded by your current circumstances. The world will once again open up to you... and so will the path that will lead you to the direction you truly want to go.

3 - *Fill Your Life With Energy!*

There was a time in my life when I found myself consumed by a failed relationship. I barely had any energy to take care of myself, much less to work with gusto — like I'd usually do. I felt like I was floating in mid-air, simply letting the wind take me wherever it pleased.

But at the same time, I felt heavy as a rock. The weight of my predicament made it really difficult for me to socialise, show joy, or even think in a positive and constructive way. As a result, I felt all the other aspects of my life crumble. I couldn't be productive, so of course, the quality of my work suffered, as did my capacity to earn. I couldn't stand being around happy people, so I ended up disconnecting with a lot of my friends. I couldn't even eat and sleep right, so of course, my health started to falter.

Needless to say, that dark time in my life almost broke me.

Fortunately for me, what people say about time healing all wounds turned out to be true.

Slowly, I started getting back on my feet. I finally accepted the fact that the relationship simply didn't work out... and started moving forward. And so one by one, the other aspects of my life also started to recover. My work, my relationships with other people, and my health all started to mend with me.

And that's when I realised that the energy I put out in the world... was the main thing responsible for what I attracted back into my life. When I had barely any energy to share with the people and things around me, I attracted one bad thing after another. But when I regained my positive energy and started projecting this out into the world... I likewise attracted good, positive things back into my life.

That's why I've made energy a key part of what I give out into the world... and of what I seek out from the company I keep.

So, when I look for clients to work with and teams engage with… I take the time to FEEL their energy. I know us human beings are like sponges that absorb the energies of what surrounds us… and so I've learned to be careful about the kind of energy I'm letting into my personal and professional life.

Just like an eagle will never eat a dead animal… I never engage with people who give off negative energy… or no energy at all!

I mean… I've been there.

I know I've wasted so much time and energy in my life on people and opportunities that only drained the life out of me… instead of energising my soul to fly high and be strong like an eagle.

But that's all in the past.

I've bid goodbye to the people and things in my life which do not fill me with joy and energy. And I've since replaced them with people and things that inspire and energise me to be better.

And now I urge you to do the same.

Fill your life with things and people that fill you with excitement and energy… as surrounding yourself with 'lifeless' things will deplete you of your own life force… and prevent you from being at your best.

4 - Let the STORM Lift You Up!

How do you like it when it's raining outside?

How about when it's *storming* outside?

When *I* think about the many storms that brewed during my career as an aspiring Project Management Professional… I can't say I enjoyed walking through them. In fact, there were many times when I did retreat as a natural instinct and survival response.

But even then, I knew that ALL of my personal and professional growth would come from weathering those STORMS.

Indeed, not only have I discovered things about myself that I would have never discovered if I walked exclusively on dry land... but I also developed a strong belief in myself... that has lifted my self-confidence into the stratosphere.

So, remember that storms are inevitable. Be it in business, or your personal life.

And when those storms do come, you have two options:

Either you get so good at avoiding these storms, that you don't end up where you really want to go... or you learn to navigate through the storm and come out the other side stronger, more resilient, and exactly where you want to be.

The question is... what would the eagle inside you choose to do?

Of course, it's the latter.

As you know, eagles get excited when a storm is brewing. Not only do they love the challenge... but they've pretty much mastered the art of leveraging the energy of the storm... to lift themselves up... and fly high with minimal effort. In other words, they see the storm as an opportunity to rest their wings.

Isn't that just amazing?

Meanwhile, the rest of us frequently miss the opportunities that storms bring... because we get much too focused on avoiding these challenges.

As a result, we're like chickens who take cover when it's raining... while the eagle spreads its large wings... and prepares to take advantage of the strong winds so as to soar to greater heights

So, to unleash the eagle within you... be sure to leverage challenges to learn new skills, become stronger and grow holistically as an individual. And as you weather the STORMS, never forget to spread your wings and allow the situation to lift you up... and go with relative ease to where you want to go.

5 - Don't Let Complacency Kill Your Potential

"The tragedy of life is often not in our failure, but rather in our complacency; not in our doing too much, but rather in our doing too little; not in our living above our ability, but rather in our living below our capacities."

- *Benjamin E. Mays*

Let's cut to the chase and talk about something you and I have both done at least once in our lives.

I'm talking about getting comfortable and taking a back seat in life.

Why drive when you can sit on the bus and enjoy the scenery, right?

Well, you could do that for sure… but I want you to know that falling victim to complacency has the potential to be the biggest killer of your dreams. It can hold you back from having a full and rewarding existence on this planet.

I know this, because at one stage, I let myself be complacent while running my IT Support & Consulting business.

Things in the business were running on autopilot. Money was flowing. There was a lot of work and opportunities… and life was just so sweet.

And so I thought… "Let me just close my eyes for a moment and let my team take over so I could sit back and get some rest."

I started losing one or two clients… and I didn't mind. My profits began to dip a bit… and I reckoned it was fine. Some team members jumped ship… and I let them.

Until the Global Financial Crisis slapped me in the face.

I've told you this before… but let me just reiterate that my complacency during the time prior to the crash.. almost cost me my business and my relationship.

All because I allowed myself to get too comfortable…

…which is something an eagle would never do.

See, the mother eagle prepares a nest where its eggs can comfortably lay. But when it's time for the eaglets to learn how to fly... the mother eagle will begin to remove the comfort layers from the nest, exposing the uncomfortable sticks underneath.

But that's not all.

At some point, the mother eagle will then throw the eaglets out of the nest to force it to learn how to fly. This process of throwing the eaglets out of the nest is repeated... until the eaglet eventually gets stronger with each flap of its wings... and then starts to fly effortlessly.

So, just like the eagle family that goes through the tedious process of throwing eaglets out the nest until they learn how to fly... we must learn never to be complacent in life.

I know it's easy to settle into a routine and cling to the old and familiar. But as I've mentioned several times in this book... some of the best things in life may be found when you step out of your comfort zone. That means you've got to take every opportunity to reject complacency and instead work on continuously improving yourself.

Just like the eagle who goes through great pains in order to learn how to soar and fly high... so must you take full responsibility for your individual growth and personal development. And if you have someone in your life who is willing to "throw you off the nest," don't dismiss them outright as an enemy. Let me tell you that sometimes, tough love is best. Perhaps, that one person in your life who always challenges you... just doesn't want you to spend your entire life in *your* nest.

6 - Recharge Your Batteries Often!

Let me tell you what happened after the Great Financial Crisis almost took me down because of my own complacency:

I tried to overcorrect... and swung right to the opposite — and equally dangerous — end of the spectrum.

I'm talking about working until I'm running on fumes. I got so scared of being complacent... that I ended up being a workaholic. I'm talking sitting in front of my computer until the wee hours of the morning, skipping breakfast, and then heading straight to work on four hours of sleep or less. And I took this unhealthy habit to a whole new level when I entered the Project Delivery Space.

I'm sure you've observed that as Project Management Professionals... we know how to work hard and burn that midnight oil. Especially when we're in the throes of a critical and complex project implementation... and it's all hands-on deck. During these times, we gain a tendency to remove anything that could distract us from work... and many times this would include good things, as well. Like time spent for rest and recreation.

I remember preparing to launch a new core network as part of a tech project my technical team had been planning for months. It all came down to this one all-nighter involving a cast of what seemed like hundreds... who came together to do final checks and reviews before project implementation. I can vividly recall looking around the room and realising every single person in that room sacrificed time away from family and friends... rejected the pleasures of relaxation... rejected the nourishment our bodies and souls needed by eating junk... deprived themselves of proper sleep... and missed gym time... for months leading to that one night.

Clearly, I started to see the impact these unhealthy habits were having on all of us. Sure, the team eventually succeeded in transitioning to the new core network infrastructure seamlessly... but all the hard work we put in definitely took its toll on the team. I got scared that I might be jeopardising my health and life... in the interest of doing a great job at work.

I decided that wasn't a fair trade...

So, right after the project was completed successfully, I started consciously setting aside time to recharge my batteries. I stopped making every excuse not to take some time out for myself to recharge... finally realising that recharging my batteries is critical to having a full and happy life.

After all, even the mighty eagle knows how to tap out when it needs to.

See, despite the strength of an eagle... the condition of its body begins to deteriorate as it reaches the age of 30 to 40 years. So, in order for it to survive and regain its strength... the eagle flies way up to a mountaintop for a retreat... which could apparently last for about five months! During that time, their physical body undergoes a metamorphosis... which ultimately gives the eagle enough strength to continue living mightily for another thirty to forty years.

Isn't that amazing?

I do hope that when the demands of your work or life start to drain you of your life energy... you follow the eagle's example and make time for a retreat so you could recharge your batteries.

And when I talk about recharging your batteries, I'm not talking about taking the kids swimming or going out with your partner... although those things definitely deserve time out of your schedule, too. I'm also not talking about just sleeping... though you do need to maintain healthy sleeping patterns.

What I mean when I say recharge your batteries... is doing something you're passionate about. Something that makes you feel alive. It may be a hike in the mountains, a day in the wineries, or taking that much-needed trip to Europe for a couple of weeks. And do it as often as you need to regain your joy and passion for life.

7 - Rebirth Should Be Your Focus

Some of the most successful and inspirational people on this planet have transformed and rebirthed themselves.

Arnold Schwarzenegger changed careers twice. First, he transitioned from being a 20-year-old world-champion bodybuilder to being a world-class actor in his 30s. Second, he turned to politics and became the Governor of California in 2003 at 56.

Ronald Reagan was a young, up-and-coming Hollywood actor before he became the 40th president of the United States at 69.

Martha Stewart was a full-time model before becoming a stockbroker. And after a five-year stint on Wall Street, Stewart used her love for cooking... to build what is now known as Martha Stewart Living Omnimedia.

I personally believe I am a completely different person than who I was as a young adult. The life I have led... the people I have interacted with... the communities I have been a part of... the jobs which I have held... the business activities I have undertaken... the losses and challenges in my life... the people whom I have been inspired and motivated by... and the multitude of mistakes I have made... have all allowed me to be reborn many times... until I became what I am today.

And just like Janet in The Good Place, I have come back stronger, smarter, and better with each rebirth.

But I am nowhere near done being reborn.

I am rebirthing myself even as I write this book! This literally means realising my own vision for who I need to become next.

See, who you are and where you are today is NEVER a reflection of everything that's in store for you in the future. But the challenging part of being reborn... is embracing just how painful and uncomfortable it could be.

What do I mean by that?

Well, I've told you about the five-month retreat the eagles go on... in order to extend their lives for another 30 years, right?

Now, it's time for you to find out what the eagle does with all its time up on that mountain top.

Ready?

During its retreat, the eagle goes through the painful task of breaking its own beak... and plucking out its feathers, so that new ones could grow. Sounds ghastly, I know, but that's exactly what the eagle needs to do to complete its retreat — or its rebirth.

I'm sure you've heard the phrase — "No pain, no gain."

Truer words have never been spoken.

Many of us want success. A transformative journey. A complete change in who we are and how we live. But very few are willing to face the sacrifice, hard work, and heart-break that comes with being reborn.

Now, if you are determined to change your life, you must celebrate the death of your old self... and welcome your rebirth.

Yes, it sounds drastic, metaphoric, and a little bit morbid... but the brutal reality is that you need to decide from today forward to:

- End the toxic relationships in your life
- Leave the toxic jobs you have
- Eliminate your destructive habits
- Replace your negative thoughts with positive ones
- Transform your limiting beliefs by surrounding yourself with people who believe in you
- Create new rituals and traditions in your life that enhance your being
- And reprogram your mindset to SERVE you unboundedly

8 - Remember the Aspiring Youth!

Everyone knows eagles are mighty and unyielding. Predatory and unrelenting. Strong and powerful.

But did you know eagles are actually very caring and attentive... when it comes to their young ones?

That's a little known fact about eagles... but it is supported by much research.

We've talked about mother eagles and their practice of throwing eaglets off their nest to teach them how to fly... right?

Well, let's talk about it some more.

Because while this practice is pretty well-known among birds... there is more than meets the eye in how eagles teach their young how to fly.

See, mother eagles don't simply chuck their young off the nest. Instead, they fly into the air with an eaglet on their back. And when the eaglet least expects it, they will find themselves without their mother under them... after which they will have to begin flying. The whole time, the mother is always there, ready to catch them. This process is repeated until the eaglets can reliably fly on their own.

I think of my parents in this context.

When I was young, they were there to nurture me and help me learn quickly from my mistakes. But they also pushed me by giving guided challenges throughout my early life.

So too should we take the time to invest in the Aspiring Youth in our proximity... to share with them the insights that we have learned. At the same time, we must strive to protect them from the pitfalls that we've experienced ourselves.

Take the case of one of my dear friends, Eric Agyeman. Today, people know him as an empowering Youth Mentor.

But those of us who knew him as a child know he has experienced a whole lot. We know he was a victim of racial bullying in primary school... got expelled in high school... became a gang member... and dealt with depression and anger issues.

Two decades later, Eric dedicated his life to giving the YOUTH around him what he did not have when growing up. That's exactly why he founded The Royal Hood... a Christian mentoring program for young people. Eric's mission is to reach and empower a million young people and their families... to position them for their best possible future together.

See? Great people know the importance of investing in the younger generation. So, as you take on the role of being life mentors for your children or the children of others at work or otherwise... you mustn't forget to empower and direct them the right way. Start by giving them daring yet reasonable challenges to help them grow.

Through this process of helping young people around you grow... you will also attain growth and personal development for yourself.

Remember the mother eagle and their aspiring young!

Stop Holding Yourself Back

"Celebrate your success and stand strong when adversity hits, for when the storm clouds come in, the eagles soar while the small birds take cover"

- Napoleon Hill

As you've learned from this chapter, the eagle is a majestic creature that deserves emulation.

Unfortunately, the same isn't true for the eagle who was brought up as a chicken... and got trapped into that life.

Interestingly, many people will hear the story of the eagle who grew up around chickens. A lot of those people will even feel bad for the eagle who got stuck... and never realises its potential. But strangely, only a handful of those people will work hard to save themselves from the same situation... when they fall victim to it.

So, ask yourself this:

What is holding you back from realising that there's an eagle inside you waiting to be found and released?

Are you taking the wait-and-see approach?

Because if you are, you'll eventually stop seeing opportunities to be an eagle. You will become fully convinced that you are a chicken... until you entirely lose the ability to soar and be mighty.

So, when an opportunity to call on the eagle inside you comes... pay close attention. And once you feel that your inner eagle is ready to burst out and start soaring... don't hold back.

Don't wait for that perfect moment... as it may never come.

Remember: perfect moments are made by YOU!

CHAPTER 10

It's All in Your Mindset

Let me share with you a mind-blowing fact that's true for most people... but only very few are aware of:

The average person doesn't make a conscious decision before 10 am.

I don't mean to say we don't make *any* decisions from the time we wake up until the clock hits 10. What I'm saying is that most of those early morning decisions are made by our subconscious minds.

Come to think about it...

Every day, I get up. I put on clothes. I make and eat breakfast, take a shower, brush my teeth, and prepare to leave for work.

All these activities involve microdecisions... but they all happen at such an automatic level that I'm almost on autopilot.

Isn't the same true for you?

And when you get in the car... do you realise that the level to which your subconscious mind takes control goes even higher? You could be daydreaming about absolutely anything. You could be replaying what happened at work the last time you were there... or thinking about what you'd be having for dinner...

Which means it's your subconscious mind that's driving.

Then, after your 25-minute commute, you arrive at work.

You don't even realise that you've changed lanes 15 times, stopped at all the red lights, overtaken safely at all the right times.

Not a single conscious decision was made in those 25 minutes... and yet you arrive at work safe and in one piece.

As a result, you make it to your 10am standup... and only then does your conscious mind take over to make your first real decisions of the day.

Isn't it crazy how powerful our subconscious can be?

And this is not just true on a micro, day-to-day scale.

See, in 2004, I formally left my last full-time role with Qantas Airways. Fast forward 19 years later, I'm a Project Management Professional writing this book to share with you everything I know about this profession and the key learnings I have had.

I am worlds away from who I used to be and the life I used to have.

And at times, I still find myself asking: *How did I even get here?*

But I know the answer to that one:

I am where I am today... as a result of a thousand little decisions I've made along the way. And the fact that I couldn't possibly list down all those micro-decisions tells me... my subconscious must have played a gigantic role in all of this, again.

Truly, our subconscious minds do most of the work for us... we don't even realise how much our lives have changed because of the decisions it's made.

I mean, if you try to look back on all the things that have happened in your life so far... would you be able to guess how much of it took place because of your subconscious mind?

40%? 50%? 75%?

Well, research tells us it's much more than that. In fact, scientific studies estimate that 95 percent of our lives are controlled by our subconscious minds. That's because 95 per cent of our brain's activity happens unconsciously. Meaning, the majority of the decisions we make, the actions we take, as well as the emotions and behaviours we exhibit... depend on the 95 percent of brain activity that lies beyond our conscious awareness.

And that only means one thing:

We've got to have our subconscious minds working for us. Otherwise, we would never get to where it is that we want to go.

See, you can drive to work easily on autopilot... because your subconscious mind knows where to go. It knows what time you have to be at the office. And it knows that it has to get you there safely.

But does your subconscious mind know where you're going on a macro scale? Are your goals as a Project Management Professional imprinted deep enough in your subconscious? Can you confidently say your subconscious will make all the right microdecisions that will make you the kind of person and professional you're working hard to be?

Because if the answer is no, or that you don't know...

Then you and I have got our work cut out for us.

We've got to ensure that your subconscious is working in your favour... and is not making any decisions that will hinder you from reaching your goals.

And to be able to do all that, you've got to harness the power of your subconscious mind... first and foremost by understanding exactly how it works.

Three Important Facts About the Subconscious Mind

There are three important things you should know about the subconscious mind:

#1. It's primal.

Our subconscious minds do not depend on reason. It takes in information through images, feelings, and stories. That means it creates decisions based on emotion and gut feel... instead of logic or reason.

What we know as intuition is actually our subconscious mind sending signals to our conscious mind... without providing any analytical reasoning as to why it reacts, thinks, or wants you to act a certain way.

#2. It's ALWAYS awake.

The subconscious mind *never* takes a break. It doesn't rest or sleep… as it practically controls all our vital processes and bodily functions. It controls our heartbeat, blood circulation, and even our digestion. I mean, you don't do any of those things consciously, do you?

Even in sleep where our conscious mind becomes dormant and takes a rest… our subconscious mind stays fully awake… sometimes communicating things to us through dreams. That's why people say a dream is a wish your heart makes.

#3. It takes EVERYTHING literally.

As Henry Ford once put it:

"If you think you can, or if you think you can't… you're right!"

This is probably the most important thing you have to understand about your subconscious. It cannot differentiate between negative and positive. That means it's unable to discard any of the information it gets… on the basis of it being wrong, negative, or even harmful.

It simply takes it all in without independent reason or prejudice. And the more times it gets the same information… the more it starts to mark it as the truth. Which is why it's so difficult to unlearn some of the things our parents kept on repeating to us as we were growing up.

In fact, if you want to make way for new learnings that are inconsistent with what your subconscious mind has already marked as truth… you've got to make a *conscious* effort to unlearn old beliefs to make way for new ones.

I remember growing up with my parents who encouraged me to take risks fearlessly. Because of the way they brought me up, I subconsciously gained a belief that the best way to learn was to try as many times as I needed for me to get something right… even if it means making a dozen different mistakes first.

It wasn't until I went to school that I was exposed to a different structure of learning. This was when I discovered the concept of pass/fail. Apparently, in school, you don't always get the chance to keep trying when you get it wrong the first time. What you get instead is a failing grade and a tonne of negative judgement about your shortcomings. So, I consciously had to unlearn my fearless ways to conform to this academic standard of passing and failing. Soon, my subconscious mind started avoiding failures and mistakes... as a way to help my conscious mind survive in school.

But then later on in life, I realised that school didn't always get it right. I once again rediscovered the value in failing as many times as it takes to succeed. This meant I had to consciously recall my old mindset and re-learn how to to stop fearing failure... until my subconscious mind regained its preference for exploration and risk-taking.

And that's just one instance in my personal life where I had to harness the power of my subconscious mind... in order to make it work in my favour.

Now, because of all those instances of unlearning, learning, and re-learning things... I have become more aware of how my subconscious works. In fact, I've found that I am able to influence my subconscious when I need to... instead of always leaving it in the driver's seat.

Thus, self-awareness has become a skill I've adopted as part of my daily existence.

And since I believe one of the most wonderful gifts we could give each other is the sharing of experiences and learnings... whether good or bad... I'd love to share with you the eight greatest lessons I've learned from continuously harnessing my subconscious mindset.

8 Greatest Lessons that Drove My Growth Mindset

1. Most of the problems you will face in life will eventually come to pass

As the old adage goes: *"This, too, shall pass."*

I've told you before about one of the worst challenges I've come to face in this life. It was when my first marriage failed. As you already know, at the time it felt like my whole world was falling apart. Things got so bad I even

155

started questioning my own self-worth and often wondered if it was even possible to recover from that kind of pain.

My subconscious mind, who had spent the last few years in a loving, committed marriage, was convinced I would never be as happy as I was... when I was someone's husband. But because I was determined to move forward in my life, I consciously made the effort to push through all the emotions... and slowly came to terms with my situation. So, I was able to change my mindset from thinking, "I can't move forward" to wondering: "What's next for me?"

I've been through hell and back. At one point, it felt like my soul could die... but I survived to tell the tale. That's why I can look you in the eye and tell you that indeed, everything comes to pass. Even the worst days will eventually become a distant memory of a point in time that you can hopefully look back on with fondness... and learn a great deal from.

2. If you don't believe in yourself, nobody else will

Believing in yourself when everything's going well is easy. But let's be honest... believing in ourselves while we're struggling is a different kind of beast.

Still, it is during these moments that you have to keep the strongest belief in yourself. This is when you should be more conscious of your internal dialogue... because the things you tell yourself, over and over again, get imprinted in your subconscious. And since your subconscious is responsible for 95 per cent of your world... your inner dialogue ultimately plays a huge role in the kind of life you live.

So, it doesn't matter how bad things get. You still can't wake up in the morning thinking to yourself:

"I'm a loser, I'm a loser, I'm a loser."

Because if you do that... your subconscious mind will eventually clock that in as truth. And what will it do to avoid cognitive dissonance?

It will make decisions that will support its newfound truth... that you are a loser. In effect, it won't take long before you find yourself thinking, speaking, and ultimately behaving as a loser. And when everyone around you sees that... well then they'd lose confidence in you. Soon, everyone will agree that you are, indeed, a loser.

This is why you have to develop the courage to believe in yourself even in the worst of times. This is why you've got to keep talking yourself up… even if it's just in your internal dialogue. This is why you've got to make affirmations like: *"I got this. I am capable of getting through this. I will succeed."* This way, you train your subconscious to make all the right decisions to make these affirmations a reality.

And when things seem incredibly dire, remember the wise words of Winston Churchill:

"Courage is going from failure to failure without losing enthusiasm"

3. **When you create meaningful connections with others, you will earn the kind of support that helps lift you up when you need it**

"The most important things in life are the connections you make with others"

- Tom Ford

I have long made the conscious decision to surround myself with wonderful people.

And those people are few and far in between… I make sure to hold on to great connections when I do find them.

As a Project Management Professional, you have the incredible opportunity to make thousands of connections with different people. Soon, you'd find that it's not uncommon to have meetings with your stakeholders over lunch or coffee. But what you have to understand is that these nice interactions… need not only happen when you need to talk to someone about your project.

In fact, I'd like to ask you:

When was the last time you invited a friend or colleague for a coffee just to catch up… with no strings attached?

When was the last time you called someone just to have a casual chat and see how they are going?

When was the last time you dropped by someone's place just to see if they're up for something fun?

For many of us, I am sure the answer is "not for some time now".

Well, we've got to fix that!

I have learned that surrounding yourself with people who could genuinely wish you well when you're doing something good... or candidly call you out when you're doing something destructive is crucial to success.

And you can only have such kinds of friends and colleagues... if you cultivate real, authentic connections with the people around you.

So, take the time to create real relationships with people who you know could lift you up... and help you become a better person.

4. Success is built on hard work not luck

Let's be real.

Being in the right place at the right time can sometimes contribute to your success. But you can't solely rely on luck without putting in your share of hard work. In fact, if you don't get out there and do the work, you'd be missing out on every opportunity to get lucky.

Remember what that professional golfer Gary Player said?

"The more I practise, the luckier I get."

Personally, I grew up with hard-working, middle-class parents, who knew how to roll up their sleeves and work hard.

That's why the concept of working hard is programmed into my DNA.

To this day, I give 110% to all that I do. Not just because I enjoy my profession, but because I ultimately believe that success comes from working tirelessly and committing yourself to achieving whatever it is that you've set out to achieve.

See, when you work hard, you're taking control of your own destiny... leaving nothing to chance or luck. When you work hard, you declare to the universe that you're not average and that you want — and deserve — your share of the pie.

And when you get into the habit of working hard to achieve your dreams…
your subconscious mind will support you in making great decisions that
ultimately lead to your success.

**"When you want to succeed as bad as you want to breathe, then you'll
be successful."**

- Eric Thomas

5. Doing the same thing every day and expecting different results is definitely an insane way of living

I'm convinced that coming up with this quote is the main reason why Albert
Einstein is considered a genius.

Kidding aside…

Have you ever felt that no matter what you do, nothing seems to change in
your life?

You wake up each day, get the kids out of bed and shower, have your
breakfast with family and head off to work. You come back home after
work, and before you retire for the night… you desperately wish for things
to change for you soon.

But come the next day, you do the exact same things all over again.

That's just insanity.

One way or another, you'd have to accept that you're the only person who
has the full capacity to change your life. You have to accept that where you
are now is simply the result of how you've been living life… and what
things you've been focusing on.

I know I spent a good portion of my life being complacent and not really
moving forward.

It wasn't until I took responsibility for my own feelings of stagnation… that
I was able to adjust my mindset and my behaviour. And only then did I start
to get different results.

So, remember that in order to transform your life… you need to DISRUPT
your world and shift your actions in a way that propels you forward.

6. The road less travelled might seem scary, but it might be the path to your success

The world is a crowded place.

And many of us feel safe and comfortable blending in with that massive crowd.

After all, we've been taught from a young age that there is just one way to secure our futures: study well, land a great job, climb the corporate ladder, and work hard until it's time to retire.

And true enough, many professionals have lived comfortable enough lives following this formula.

But let me ask you:

Would you be happy standing at the foot of that ladder... knowing you'd just be getting the same results as everyone else that came before you?

If not, well...

You'd be glad to know that there are other pathways available to you.

But there is one problem.

Most of them have never been walked on before. And that makes them downright terrifying. Would you then dare to pave the way on one of these less-travelled roads? Or would you rather walk on the main road... where everything is safe and predictable?

A philosophy I have adopted is to at least keep an open mind to the many roads and doorways which are available to us in life.

After all, it is up to you to choose which roads to walk on and which doors to walk into.

But what I can tell you is that I never would have achieved the amazing life I'm living today... if I didn't *always* take the road less travelled.

Remember, you may take the old, familiar, and crowded path to be rewarded with a life of comfort. Or you could choose to be adventurous and set out on a scary, sometimes lonesome journey... and be rewarded with extraordinary greatness.

The choice is yours.

"I took the road less travelled by, and that has made all the difference."

– Robert Frost

7. FEAR is normal, but if something is important to you enough, you can work through even your worst fears

There have been so many times in my own life where I felt fear.

When I did my first open water dive. When I first voiced my opinion in a public forum. And whenever I have to get up in front of a crowd to speak.

It's funny, though, because all these things I mentioned... these are things I know I'm pretty good at. And not only that — these are things I actually enjoy doing!

So, why so much fear?

Perhaps fear is just inevitable. But I am more inclined to believe that fear is mostly just self-induced. After all, it's only your perception of what could happen... that creates fear in you. In any case, fear sometimes consumes us to the point of preventing us from going after our most daring goals and dreams.

You have likely been confronted by similar situations before.

There's so much out there you know you're capable of attaining... but for some reason, your fears get in the way. It holds you back, until some of the best opportunities pass you by without you grabbing them.

That's why I believe that fear is the biggest deterrent to success.

So, if you want to make the most of your life, you've got to challenge your fears.

Look your fears straight in the eye and commit to conquering them boldly. Promise yourself that you won't let a self-induced feeling stand in the way of you and your biggest dreams.

The day you decide to stand up and push back against fear... is the day that your life changes forever. There's nothing more fulfilling than overcoming what scares you the most... and gaining that confidence to keep doing it and move   forward.

161

8. Be BOLD and take some risks

We all have different risk appetites.

At the end of the day, it's a personal decision how much risk you're willing to take with your life, your future and your money.

But here's what you have to understand:

The higher your ambitions are, the more risk you'd have to take to get them.

For example…

The ambitions of a project manager are different from those of a salesperson. Just like the ambitions of a salesperson are different from those of an entrepreneur. And with each different level of ambition comes a different level of risk… and a different level of reward. As we know, the higher the risk, the higher the reward.

Now, I know your ambitions are way high.

But you don't have to be scared of all the risks you've got to take.

Just to put things in perspective, let me just tell you that from the minute we were born, we are already exposed to a million different risks. Even just being born is risky in itself! The sooner you can realise and accept this, the faster your perspective about risk could change.

Personally, I've stopped minding risks so much. Because if you think trying new things is risky… wait until you get the bill for not trying.

And besides, there is not one thing in this world that you can do… that doesn't involve taking risks. Getting married is risky. Going into business is risky. Even crossing the road is risky. But should that stop us from doing any or all those things?

You tell me!

"It's really not important how long we live, but more so HOW we live!"

CHAPTER 11

Your Life's Adventure Awaits

The most beautiful thing about life... is that you can make it whatever you want to be.

Life's an adventure, after all. And every day is a new beginning — a new chance to choose what you want to focus on... in order to fulfil whatever destiny you'd like to have for yourself.

You know what that means, right?

It means you're not bound to whatever has happened in your past. What happened yesterday will never be representative of what happens tomorrow. Because from the moment you wake up in the morning, you can make the conscious choice to do things differently this time around.

I've told you about my upbringing and how I had to work hard to overcome all the BRULES I was taught from a young age.

I've told you about the time I almost lost my identity for the kind of person my "friends, work, and society" wanted me to be... and how I stopped walking amongst chickens so I can soar high like an eagle.

I've told you about the time I pulled myself out of the clutches of burnout by shaking off the highway hypnosis and taking better control of my daily decisions.

These personal experiences are all proof that you can change the course of your own adventure... at any point in your life. Because if I can get up and create a new beginning for myself so many times in what has been a relatively short timespan... then there's no reason why you can't do the same.

So if you're feeling stuck where you are right now, know that you have the power to get yourself unstuck. You can choose to exist however you want to exist in this world. And you can start by searching for the happiness you so deserve... which is already within you... along with the many secret powers residing in you... that are just waiting to be released to the world.

But since changing your destiny may be easier said than done... and because I've somehow done it more times already than some do in their lifetimes... I'd love to share with you four fundamental principles which I personally apply to everything I do in my own life:

1 - Create a sense of ADVENTURE in your life

Many of us tend to feel like we have no real purpose in life. Or that we have no real focus day to day. This leads to a lot of unhappiness, discontentment, and running around in circles.

I, too, remember those moments in my own life where I was stuck in the "rat race." As you already know, I found myself doing the same thing day in and day out — wake up, eat breakfast (or miss it), go to work, do a day's work, come home, have dinner, watch some TV, spend some time with the family, go to bed... and then do it all again the next day.

There were some good moments, for sure, but when you live repetitively like that... life can become so unsatisfying. When your main focus becomes paying the bills, taking care of the family, and just generally doing the grind, it can be all-consuming.

That's why it's very important that you inject some sense of adventure in your life. Here are some ways you can do just that:

1. Unleash your curiosity

This is the first step to developing a more adventurous spirit. Instead of spending all your time at home, decide to use your weekend to discover more of the world. Start with your local area... and once you get the hang of having these new adventures... try exploring somewhere unknown to you. Just get out there and roam freely — this is the best way to unleash your curious mind. Even just taking a different route to work can add some adventure into your daily life.

2. Try new things that will allow you to learn new skills

It would be a great tragedy to leave this physical world without having discovered all the treasures within us. And it is a fact that you will NEVER know what you are capable of... until you take a leap of fate and try new things. For this reason, those of us whose skills remain undeveloped generally underestimate the skills that we do have within us... and never reveal what we could do with them. So, make it your mission to get out and try different things often. Engaging in sports, hobbies, or even getting involved with organisations who can help you unearth your hidden talents.

3. Seek new knowledge every day

We've already discussed how your beliefs drive your daily habits and actions. Now, I want you to understand that seeking new knowledge every day is a wonderful way of being. See, gaining new knowledge shapes better beliefs... which in turn drives healthier habits and more productive actions. Remember that learning doesn't stop after school or university; in fact, the school of life is where all the real learning begins. One way to be a daily knowledge seeker is to mix up what you would normally watch, read, and consume. By opening up your mind to new learnings, you can overcome your own limiting beliefs and mental blocks... and embark on a transformational adventure that can change your destiny.

4. Help others more

Lastly, and possibly the greatest adventure you can take on in this life... is helping others. Immersing yourself in someone else's world challenges your skills, beliefs, and capacity to understand more of the world around you. As such, helping others can be a rewarding and fulfilling life adventure.

With that, I'd love for you to take control of your world and create your own adventures... by getting out there and making every day an extraordinary chance to explore, experiment, experience and grow.

2 - Realise that YOU'RE in control of your OWN life

The moment you realise that you're in control of your own life... can be a huge turning point to a whole new world that's been waiting for you.

Throughout my life, there have been many times when I felt that life was taking ME for a ride. As if it's controlling me, instead of the other way around. I'm pretty sure you've felt the same way before. And perhaps, during those moments, you get the urge to complain and blame all things external to you that are out of your control. Basically, you blame everyone and everything else for what's happening in your life.

But by now, you should already know that it is your inner self that determines how exactly you choose to live life. Sure, all of us were born with a certain set of circumstances which may initially prevent us from achieving the things we want. But through Personal and Professional Self-Mastery... we can overcome those circumstances to turn our lives around. Until you review your personal, professional, and spiritual life... as well as acknowledge your beliefs, strengths and weaknesses... it could be very difficult for you to take control of your own life.

What makes things more challenging is the fact that taking control of your own life requires us to leave our comfort zone. After all, it's much easier to just go with the flow — to just let other people and circumstances define who we are and what we can do with our lives. But if you truly want to be in the driver's seat of your own life... you've got to get out of the comforts of the passenger seat. That's exactly what I did when I signed up for my first formal personal development training with my own coach, Scott Harris.

Now, here are some of my most important takeaways from that experience... which I think can also help you in taking control of your world:

1. Be more aware of how you are living

The first thing you have to take control of is your own beliefs and behavioural patterns. To do that, you need to acknowledge all your current beliefs and behaviours. Yes, introspection may indeed be scary as you'll never know what you could discover... but this is the first step you need to take in order to move forward.

2. Surround yourself with the right people

As Les Brown puts it — QPO. Quality People Only. Being surrounded by positive people is paramount to taking control of your life. Remember: you don't want to be walking amongst chickens if what you want is to soar like an eagle. So, take a good look at the people you spend most of your time with. You might find — like I did — that you have some negative people in your life… that may be trying to control or influence you in a negative way. If so, replace them with people who support you in all your dreams and aspirations… and those who believe that you can indeed take control of your own life.

3. Make the decision to take control of your own life — no ifs, no buts

When I made the decision to shift careers and take control of my life without excuses, that's when the tables started to turn for me. I suddenly had a multitude of choices which originally did not present themselves… because of my limited thinking and world view. So, if you think it's time to dive into a new career in Project Management, tell the universe you're ready. Surrender to its powers and it will surely support you through your own journey.

4. Get moving by doing

Earlier, I told you to gain some new skills by trying out new things more often. Well, as you take control of your own life, you've got to put those new skills into action. After all, our skills diminish every second that we don't use them. So, get moving by doing… and give yourself every opportunity to unlock the full potential of those skills you've picked up along the way.

5. Believe in yourself

Even though you may not have all the things you need right now… you still have the power within you to take charge of your life. As you develop your consciousness, hold the vision of what you want to do. And as you decide to answer the voices from within… you will soon attract the right ideas and people that will allow you to achieve what you want to achieve.

3 - Aim HIGH

I've always believed that aiming high and missing… is far better than aiming low and hitting.

Let me explain.

As you embark on any new adventure, you will come upon some low-hanging fruit. These are the most easily achieved of a set of tasks. They might give you temporary fulfilment... but aiming only for low-hanging fruit keeps you well within your comfort zone. It is only by working on tasks that stretch you beyond your current capabilities... that you can step out of that zone to discover and develop your best potential.

When I look at my own life and the many things I have and still am trying to achieve... I realise that most of my growth and reward has come from aiming high. Higher, indeed, than what I thought to be possible for me at a particular point in time. It is from that struggle to climb higher and achieve better things that I became who I am today. And let me tell you... I didn't always hit my marks. But aiming high and missing still transformed me for the better.

By aiming higher, I discovered five important things that helped me along my life adventure:

1. Motivation and Inspiration

No inspiration comes from collecting low-hanging fruit. It is only when you're fueled by challenges that you can draw upon the motivation and inspiration you need... to keep going beyond what you think you can achieve.

2. A Sense of Responsibility

Aiming higher than where you are today also makes you more responsible in making decisions. After all, every decision you make affects how far you can go in your life's adventure. So, if you seem to be achieving things too quickly... maybe you need to step it up and set some goals that are a little bit more challenging to accomplish. Otherwise, you might never develop the sense of responsibility that's needed to take yourself to the next level.

3. New and Creative Ideas

When you aim high, you will face many obstacles. To overcome these challenges, you can't just rely on your old ways of thinking or doing things.

168

This means you'll be forced to take your creativity to the next level. When you force the mind beyond its limits, that's when the magic really starts to take place.

4. Courage and Confidence

As Brian Tracy says: *"The comfort zone is the greatest enemy of courage and confidence."* Aiming higher takes you way beyond your comfort zone... because that's not where your dreams will come true. Sure, it's a great place to be and fall back to from time to time as it feels homely and comfortable... but if you want to see your dreams fulfilled... you've got to get moving as soon as possible.

5. Your True Potential

It's a sad reality that many of us will never realise our true potential. You can trick yourself by repeatedly saying "not yet..." but if you don't take action soon, "not yet" could very quickly turn to "never." So, aim high... because having a big dream or goal could unlock your true potential and can lead you to places you wouldn't even know existed... if you keep aiming for low-hanging fruit. After all, there's nothing bad about living small and being happy with it... but what if your life can be extraordinary? Wouldn't you want to at least experience a one-of-a-kind life?

4 - Keeping yourself HEALTHY is the cornerstone to a great adventure

When you play a game and your character loses all of its health power, what happens? You lose. You start over. You waste all your progress and return to your last saved point. Well, real life is not so different. Without great health, everything else will prove to be a challenge... and you will never be at the top of your game.

The fundamental cornerstone of being at your prime in both your personal and professional lives come down to your overall health. So, here are some tips on how you can stop neglecting your health... and start laying down a solid foundation for your personal and professional success:

1. Stay in touch with your doctor

Very few people actually like going to the doctor. Most of us only come in for a check up when something is wrong. The problem with this approach is it doesn't let us catch any issues or anomalies before they become a problem. So, be more proactive in managing your health by having regular check ups. This way, you can boost not just your lifespan, but also the quality of your life.

2. Maintain your fitness through MOVEMENT

Exercise helps keep your Body Mass Index in a healthy range... which in turn decreases your chances of suffering from illnesses like heart disease, diabetes, dementia, and even depression.

Exercise and general physical movement are also key components to helping our bodies prevent high blood pressure, joint and muscle diseases, and stress. Being physically active keeps both the body and mind strong... which is critical to being at the top of our game.

3. Get enough sleep

Sleep serves as your body's main immune system support. That makes it absolutely essential for the body and mind to function normally. Unfortunately, the average person gets only around 6 to 7 hours of sleep at night... while research has repeatedly shown that we need closer to 8 hours for our bodies and minds to reach optimal performance. Inadequate sleep will have both short-term negative effects on your body... and will prevent you from having the mental sharpness to be at the top of your game. So, always strive to find enough time for the quantity and quality of sleep that your body requires.

4. Eat more mindfully

You are what you eat, and that makes your nutrition a critical element of being at the top of your game. The sad part is that we live in a commercial world where processed foods are all that's readily available for convenience. These unhealthy foods lead to a high prevalence of migraines, insomnia, gastrointestinal disorders and even some cancers!

So, if you truly want to be at the top of your game… it's important to come back to the basics of eating as much fresh, unprocessed foods as possible. Avoiding fast food and convenient sugar treats for an energy hit is a good start. And if it can't be completely avoided, at least consume processed or unhealthy food in moderation.

5. Embrace that you are a social being

We've said time and time again that having a solid support network is integral to your success. But social wellness is not only important for your mental health and mindset. Surrounding yourself with people who influence you to have a healthier lifestyle is also critical to your health. So, instead of finding yourself some drinking buddies, why not find yourself some fitness buddies? Find friends who would love to bond with you over healthy food and weekend workouts… and you will soon find yourself immersed in a regimen that does wonders for your physical and mental health

6. Never neglect your quiet time

Mindfulness is the state of being fully aware of the present moment… while calmly acknowledging whatever you might be feeling, thinking, and experiencing at this moment.

Mindfulness practices are beneficial to our general mental well-being. With the constant demands and stresses of daily life… taking some time out to quiet your mind is an important practice that I have adopted into my own life. It's something I also recommend for you to consider.

Finding time each day to just sit and be present for that moment… can bring clarity to any situation you may be dealing with at that time. Even just five minutes of quiet, mindful time before or after a critical meeting will allow you to focus your thoughts in a constructive way… and ground you so you can be mentally in check.

Life's adventures have definitely thrown me some curveballs. And I'm sure it will bring some your way, too… but the beautiful thing about life is that you can use those curveballs to propel you forward… into a life filled with adventure and happiness.

Whether or not you eventually decide to start a career in Project Management… I hope this book has brought you value, perspective, options, opportunity, insights, inspiration and more importantly… hope.

Hope that wherever you are today... know that you have the power to transform your life and redirect it... in a way that supports the dreams and desires that you have for yourself and your loved ones.

"Your dream was given to you. If someone else can't see it for you, that's fine, it was given to you and not them. It's your dream. Hold it. Nourish it. Cultivate it!" – Les Brown

Congratulations on finishing this book!

I really hope you found it helpful, and that you were able to relate to some of the situations I personally found myself in. One thing is for sure—that the journey to success is not easy, and requires determination and persistence.

As you may already know, happiness is not a destination, either. Rather, it's more of a conscious way of being, which is enhanced through living a life of purpose and taking charge of your life overall. There will always be ups and downs along the way, but if you stay focused on your goals and maintain a "never give up" attitude, you will eventually achieve your version of success.

So let me ask you this question:

"How would YOU choose to LIVE your life if NOTHING stood in your way?"

Would you travel the world? Spend more time with friends and family? Maybe follow your passion? Or consider trying to make a difference in the world?

I believe that all of us have the potential to live a meaningful and fulfilling life. We are ALL capable of great things.

But let's be honest with ourselves. Sometimes, we just need a little help to see our potential.

If you are feeling lost or stuck in your life, as I too once was, don't let fear or doubt hold you back from potentially living your best life. So, if you are ready to take the next step, I would be honoured to work with you as your Success Coach!

I offer a variety of coaching services, working with both individuals and groups, to really disrupt and focus on how you are living your life. I pull apart your daily rituals and take a close look at the habits that you have formed so as to understand how I can help you UNLEASH your potential that is locked away inside you.

I'm super excited to discuss your needs and goals, so please visit my website at https://www.leococo.com.au/ to find out more. Remember to mention the book title **"UNLEASH the Pro in PROject Management"** for an exclusive discount for when we work together. I look forward to hearing from you!

I would also LOVE to have you as part of our wonderful community, the Project Managers Movement, so I highly recommend joining our MeetUp Community Group via this link – https://www.meetup.com/en-AU/project-managers-movement-meetup/

But, if you're really SERIOUS about transforming your world and want to surround yourself with other incredible people who have committed to their own journey towards Self-Mastery… Then consider becoming a VIP Member within the Project Managers Movement Community. Use this link with a SPECIAL discount that's exclusive to you as a reader of this book - https://tinyurl.com/unleashpropmm

In the meantime, here are a few things you can do to continue your journey towards a rewarding career in project management and a fulfilling, successful life:

- **Set clear goals and create a plan to achieve them** – this will give you purpose and pull you FORWARD in life.
- **Take action every day, no matter how small** – As the book "The Slight Edge" states, it's the little things that we do each day that will see us either progress or keep us where we are.
- **Surround yourself with positive people who will support you on your journey through life** – Who you surround yourself with will make a BIG difference to the outcome you're seeking. The lifelong relationships you create can also become part of your overall support network as well. Remember, we need GREAT people around us to help us flourish!
- **Never give up, no matter how difficult things get** – A "Do or Die" attitude, tenacity, determination, and persistence are all words that describe the mindset required to get you through life and maintain momentum.

I believe in you! You CAN achieve anything you set your mind to. So, let TODAY be the turning point for you to stop playing small.

To Your Success,

Leo Coco

Project Management Warrior | Founder of Project Managers Movement | Success Coach | Speaker | Author | Entrepreneur

Made in the USA
Columbia, SC
11 February 2025

53538383R00104